Honey Tree Publishing
www.honeytreepublishingus.com

Copyright © 2025 by Mondre Moffett
ISBN: 979-8-9990538-0-0
First Edition: Paperback

For permissions, inquiries, or more information, please contact Mondre Moffett at mondremusic@yahoo.com

Library of Congress Cataloging-in-Publication Data

Moffett, Mondre, 1953- Black Music Footprints: The Jazz Experience

1. Black American music. 2. Jazz. 3. African American History. 4. Trade.

Edited and Cover Designed by Dr. Tytianna Ringstaff

Printed in the United States of America

Contents

Acknowledgements   1

Preface   4

Introduction   7

Chapter 1   Uncharted Territory (1619-1865)   19

Chapter 2   The Blues Story (1865-1885)   26

Chapter 3   The Evolution of the Blues (1868-1917)   34

Chapter 4   The King of Ragtime (1890-1917)   45

Chapter 5   The Classic Jazz Era: The Sunburst of   54
                 Black American Culture (1900-1930)

Chapter 6   The Swing Era: A Cultural   67
                 Renaissance (1930-1940)

Chapter 7   The Bombshell of Black American   76
                 Music (1940-1960)

Chapter 8   Bebop: A Jazz Quintet Legacy (1945-1960)   103

Chapter 9   The Cool Jazz Experience: A Tale of   124
                 Two Stories (1950-1960)

Chapter 10   Avant-Garde: A Free Jazz   131
                 Movement (1960-1980)

Chapter 11   Improvisation through the Lens of   146
                 Jazz Music (1980-21st century)

Glossary   152

Bibliography   160

ACKNOWLEDGEMENTS

First and foremost, I would like to express my deepest gratitude to God for the gift of music and creativity bestowed upon me. I am humbled to be a part of a legacy shaped by my ancestors' hopes, dreams, and sacrifices.

Second, I would like to extend my sincerest appreciation to everyone who has contributed to my personal and professional growth. Your love, support, and encouragement have been invaluable to me.

I am eternally grateful to my mother, Louis Natalie Reed, for instilling in me a strong discipline in which to excel. Her legacy as an English teacher, scholar, avid reader, and church pianist and organist has instrumentally impacted my life.

I also want to acknowledge my father, Charles Mack Moffett, educator and master percussionist, who introduced me to the world of jazz and its universal language. His influence has been the primary source in shaping my musical journey.

To my maternal grandfather, James Lee Reed, I express my deepest gratitude for nurturing young musicians through his entrepreneurial spirit and hosting jam sessions at the Deluxe Hotel in Austin, Texas. These gatherings brought together future jazz luminaries, including Bertrand Adams, Ornette Coleman, Bobby Bradford, James Jordan, Marty Banks Jr., Dewey Redman, and my first formal music teacher, William Singletary.

I have been blessed with an array of musical mentors who have guided me along my journey. Thank you, Robert "Bumps" Blackwell, Clarence Avant, Quincy Jones, Bill Lee, Johnnie Coles, Dr. Eddie Henderson, Barrie Lee Hall, Fred

Wesley, Joe Henderson, McCoy Tyner, Arnett Cobb, and Grover Washington, Jr.

I have also been blessed with my spiritual mentors– Dr. J. Alfred Smith, Sr., Dr. J. Alfred Smith, Jr., Dr. Jeremiah Wright, Jr., and Dr. Kevin Wayne Cosby.

To my musical cohorts– Doug Harris, Kenny Garrett, Quentin "Rocky" White, Ron Brown, Nolan Smith, Wynton, Branford, and Delfeayo Marsalis, Stanley Jordan, Denardo Coleman, Dan Pritzker, and the entire team from the "Bolden" film– thank you for inspiring me throughout your illustrious career.

I am particularly grateful for the work and support from San Francisco State University, Long Island University, North Carolina Agricultural and Technical State University, Simmons College of Kentucky, and the Duke Ellington Orchestra.

My deepest appreciation goes to National Endowment for the Arts (NEA) jazz master and producer Todd Barkan. His unwavering commitment to the advancement of jazz music has been a source of inspiration to me.

To Dr. Tytianna Ringstaff, for your watchful editing and for being such a pleasure to work with. Thank you.

I must acknowledge the significant role that several churches have played in my musical development. The Allen Temple Baptist Church in Oakland, California, Elmwood Presbyterian Church in East Orange, New Jersey, St. James Presbyterian Church in Greensboro, North Carolina, and the St. Stephen Baptist Church family in Louisville, Kentucky, have all provided me with invaluable support and guidance.

Third, I would like to extend my sincerest appreciation to the Charles Moffett Family, specifically Shirley Moffett, and the Moffett Family Jazz Band, featuring my musical prodigy siblings– Charles Edward Moffett, Jr., Codaryl Mark

Moffett, Charisse Michelle Moffett, and the late, great Charnett "Netman" Mack Moffett. Our musical journey together has been a source of immense joy and inspiration.

On a very personal note, my heartfelt gratitude to my beloved brother, Keith Raynard Wilson, a confidant and solid rock of reason: I know you are looking down with joy from that great city of Zion.

Finally, I would like to extend my heartfelt gratitude and appreciation to my immediate family– my beautiful wife, Diane, and our children, Marchelle, Marchon, Eustacia, Jessica, Kayla, and their respective families. Your love and support have been my life anchor, and I am forever grateful. And to my grandchildren– Jeremiah, Joella, Jessica Monet, Jayla, Juliana, and Louie. You are the wind beneath my wings.

This book is dedicated to the memory of my beloved maternal grandmother, Vernie Mae Fowler Thompson, who always provided me with a personalized embroidered handkerchief to accompany me on the battlefields of intense musical explorations. Her kindness, wisdom, and generosity of spirit have been a constant source of inspiration to me.

PREFACE

The overarching idea behind writing this book is to celebrate the rich performance traditions of African American music. In this book, I pay homage to the musical giants, our ancestors– known and unknown– whom God has endowed with exceptional creativity, improvisational mastery, and a heart to serve the beloved community. Our ancestors were incredibly imaginative and skilled, creating Black American music reflecting their lives and calls for liberation and freedom. I am deeply inspired by their commitment to sharing stories of hope along the challenging journey of life. As James Weldon Johnson and J. Rosamond Johnson so eloquently express in the second verse of their iconic work, "Lift Every Voice and Sing:"

"Stony the road we trod,

Bitter the chast'ning rod,

Felt in the days when hope unborn had died;

Yet with a steady beat,

Have not our weary feet

Come to the place for which our fathers sighed?"

Johnson's wholehearted story of faith and hope is emblematic of the power of Black American music and the place from which it originates. As we move into a bright future, we must also look back and reconnect with the path that has brought us here.

I am so grateful for the musical giants I've had the privilege to work with up close and, in some cases, emulate from afar. Throughout my formative years, I received personal and private instruction from musical champions in unconventional settings. Whether traveling on a tour bus throughout Europe with the Duke Ellington Orchestra or performing on a bandstand in Memphis, Tennessee, with the renowned Stylistics, I've experienced an organic, curriculum-like practice that prepared me to tackle life's most formidable challenges.

I had the privilege of receiving invaluable instruction while working with blues giant Jimmy Witherspoon at San Francisco's historic and iconic jazz venue, Keystone Korner. Additionally, I gained valuable performance experience on numerous Chitlin' Circuit gigs throughout the southern region of the United States of America. My most impactful educational experiences extending beyond the academic walls come to mind from those moments. While the academic classroom is crucial in music education, I believe the "learn by doing" approach on the music performance stage offers a unique perspective in student learning, transitioning from theory to practice in the pursuit of musical excellence.

My first professional gig marked the beginning of my musical evolution when I was just a preteen performing urban blues in rural Texas. This experience exemplified the paradox of blues music, where bitter and sweet expressions coexist. Blues is characterized by a juxtaposition of struggle and progress, a dynamic I've come to understand and appreciate over the years.

My blues aesthetic is integral to my identity and perhaps a shared aspect of our collective experience. As Frederick Douglass forewarned, and I paraphrase: *We must not underestimate the power of agitation in the pursuit of freedom.* When listening to Black American music, particularly jazz, I believe we should remain open to both the consonant sounds of stability and the dissonant sounds of agitation, which form the fabric of our musical legacy.

In reflecting on my experiences, from Miles Davis's dressing rooms to Art Blakey's hotel rooms, a recurring theme of instruction resonates: "Blow your horn, tell your story." This invaluable guidance has enabled me to walk in the footsteps of African American artists, standing on the shoulders of giants, and carrying the legacy forward.

INTRODUCTION

As we delve deeper into the soulful journey that gave rise to African American music, we uncover the resilience and indomitable spirit of a people whose cultural identity was forged in the crucible of adversity. The roots of this musical tradition, deeply embedded in the African American experience of enslavement and survival, blossomed into a rich tapestry of sound that has shaped American music for centuries.

The early work songs and field hollers, born out of the harsh realities of slave labor, were more than just a means of communication or a way to synchronize their toil. Their vocal expressions were imbued with the stories, hopes, and collective memories of a people stripped of their freedom but not their humanity. They carried within them the echoes of African rhythms and melodies, subtly resisting the erasure of their heritage, and laying the groundwork for what would become a diverse and dynamic musical tradition.

As the years progressed, these work songs, field hollers, and subsequent Negro Spirituals evolved, interweaving with the myriad influences of American culture. With its poignant expression of sorrow and longing, the blues emerged as a powerful testament to the African American cultural experience. In these melancholic melodies and heartfelt lyrics, the soul's deep yearning for freedom and equality found a voice resonating with people across cultural and racial boundaries.

Jazz, too, emerged from this rich cultural soil, a radiant embodiment of creativity and innovation that boldly defied the boundaries of form and convention. This vibrant music spoke to the unwavering spirit of optimism, triumph over adversity, and the exuberant celebration of life in all its complexity. With its improvisational nature, jazz mirrored the communal ethos of African musical heritage, adapted and transformed by Black Americans' distinctive triumphs and challenges. With an emphasis on individual expression within a collective framework, jazz embodied the dynamic tension between personal freedom and collective participation.

Infused with uplifting spiritual fervor, Gospel music offered solace and strength, uniting communities in faith and hope. It was a reminder of the enduring power of the Negro Spirituals, of music as a source of comfort and peace in times of trouble.

During our journey through the evolution of African American music, from the fields of the Southern plantations to the urban landscapes of the North, we witness the emergence of country and urban blues, ragtime, jazz music, boogie-woogie, rhythm & blues, soul, rock & roll, hip-hop, and beyond. Each genre, while distinct, carries within it the legacy of those early expressions of freedom, hope, and resistance.

In exploring the vibrant legacy of African American music, we uncover a kaleidoscope of creative genius that has significantly defined the American musical landscape. By honoring the remarkable achievements of Black artists, we also pay tribute to the indelible mark left by their ancestors, whose cultural heritage continues to resonate and inspire. This legacy stands as evidence of music's transformative power, bridging generations and cultures while fostering hope, healing, and unity.

Pan-Africanist Marcus Garvey's words continue to resonate through the ages when he shared the importance of Black people cherishing and honoring their African heritage and cultural origin. As we explore the odyssey of African American music, we discover a badge of honor for the unconquerable heart of a people who transformed history's darkest moments into a triumphant narrative of survival and creativity. The musical legacy presented in the chapters ahead is more than just a chronicle of artistic evolution. It's a powerful affirmation of the unbreakable human spirit, a declaration that even in the face of adversity, we can create something soul-stirring that captures the very essence of our shared humanity.

In honoring the rich lineage of African American music, we discover a majestic tree with roots deeply entrenched in cultural heritage and branches that stretch towards a shared human experience. Our musical legacy sows seeds of understanding, empathy, and unity, nourishing the fertile soil of our collective humanity. It continues to flourish, inspiring and enriching us with the clarion call of perseverance, strength, and the unrelenting human spirit.

Consider the harsh reality of children and adults confined in the depths of a slave ship, chained and packed like sardines in their own waste and misery. Imagine the haunting sounds of wailing, groans, moans, shouts, personal pleas, accompanied by the pervasive chorus of sorrowful songs. It's unfathomable to quantify the strength and determination required to overcome such distress, especially when faced with the traumatic experience of slavery, unrooted and displaced across the Atlantic Ocean. Picture in your mind the unimaginable conditions on those slave ships, and listen for the heartbeat, the drum's rhythmic pulse, and the unwavering cry for freedom.

My song "Diaspora" is a poignant attempt to capture, in some small measure, the experience of enslaved Africans on their perilous journey to an unknown destination. The lyrics are as follows:

[Verse 1]

As we journey to a place

We shall come to know his grace

Traveling in a rocky boat

Bound and chained so there's no hope

[Chorus]

Da sweet sounds of sorrow

Come freedom.

Umm

[Verse 2]

I am here so let me be

In this country Tis' of Thee

Traveled in a rocky boat

Where there's love there's always hope

[Chorus]

Da sweet sounds of sorrow

Come freedom.

Umm

[Verse 3]

As we rise from this place

Dancing in my sacred space

Tell my story through my jazz

Singing the blues, I'm free at last

[Chorus]

Da sweet sounds of sorrow

Come freedom.

Umm

The Middle Passage's traumatic legacy echoes the collective memory and unbridled determination of a people. From the depths of unimaginable pain and suffering, a musical narrative emerged from this author, transforming horror into a beacon of hope and unyielding optimism. The blues, a poignant dichotomy of sorrowful sounds, encapsulates the journey, speaking to the unbreakable will to survive, finding grace in despair, and claiming freedom as an inalienable birthright against all odds.

Black American music, in all its forms, is a powerful reminder that music can be both a mirror and a lamp, reflecting our shared humanity while illuminating the path forward. In the face of extraordinary adversity, music remains a means of preserving our history, connecting the past with the present, and the ancestors with their descendants. Within its melodies, Black American music carries the stories of millions, whispering to us of endurance, sorrow, and triumphant self-determination. Through storytelling as an art form– a product of African American ingenuity and brilliance– songs are vehicles for historical memory. These songs ensure that past lessons are not forgotten but are instead used as a foundation for understanding, growth, and a relentless pursuit of liberation.

Defining Black American Music

Black American music comes to fruition in the cultural context of an oral traditional conception. Seven primary features underscore an organic curriculum performance practice encompassing the defining features in Black American music. These features include Griot/storyteller, rhythm, call-and-response, emotive expressiveness, improvisation, collective participation, and experiential learning in Black American education.

Griot/Storyteller

In the revered oral tradition of Black American music, the griot embodies the multifaceted role of storyteller, mentor, virtuoso musician, and educator. They lead the next generation on a liberating journey through the rich tapestry of Black American music, navigating the highs and lows of history, struggle, and relentless pursuit of freedom. As part of this sacred continuum, the griot identifies as a link in a long chain of storytellers, musicians, and artists who have harnessed their talents to illuminate the human condition, challenge injustice, and inspire action. Through their craft, they honor the legacy of those who came before, while forging a new path forward, nurturing the souls of those who follow.

Black American music is grounded in the ancient art of storytelling, where the storyteller's voice is a powerful tool for fostering connection, building community, and navigating life's challenges.

Rhythm

Rhythm is not just a defining feature of Black American music. Rhythm is a pulsating heartbeat uniting individuals across generations and geography, through a shared language of artistic expression and communal identity. This concept transcends the realm of mere music, embodying a way of life where unity and harmony are not just abstract ideals but lived experiences that dwell deeply within the soul.

Rhythm in Black American music represents a collective spirit, a symphony of endurance and joy that echoes through the ages, reminding us of our shared humanity and the power of art to connect and uplift. In a nutshell, rhythm is the heartbeat of Black American music and culture, beating with a unifying force and bringing people together in harmony and celebration.

Call-and-response

Call-and-Response stands out as a distinctive and defining feature of Black American music. A dynamic interplay between a lead vocalist or instrumentalist and the responding voices or instruments characterizes this feature of Black culture. This performance technique is a hallmark of various Black American music genres, from the harmonious echoes of gospel choirs to the improvisational dialogues of jazz ensembles. Call-and-Response symbolizes communal engagement, interactive participation, and reaffirming core community values. Through this mechanism, stories are told, experiences shared, and identities affirmed. Call-and-Response serves as a powerful tool to organize musical expressions for specific purposes, achieving the following:

- **Integrity**: Collaboration and mutual respect
- **Identity**: Musical form and meaning
- **Unity**: Codifying communal expression within a group

In Black American culture, the call-and-response tradition represents a value system, cultivating integrity, reciprocity, communal bonding, and cohesive structure, while promoting a sense of shared responsibility and collective expression.

Emotive Expressiveness

Black American music's expressiveness and emotional depth are rooted in African cultural traditions, where music has long served as a powerful medium for communication, celebration, mourning, and spiritual connection. This rich cultural heritage has infused Black American music with an emotive power, enabling genres like blues, soul, and gospel to offer solace, hope, and a voice to the marginalized. These genres have the extraordinary ability to touch the souls of listeners, deeply echoing their experiences and emotions.

In the final reckoning, emotive expressiveness is a sacred pillow, embodying a commitment to empathy, spiritual growth, and social justice, where the power of raw emotion is harnessed to uplift, heal, and challenge the status quo for equality.

Improvisation

Improvisation is a vital thread weaving African and Black American music together, fostering creativity and community. In African cultural traditions, improvisation enables musicians to stamp their individuality on the collective canvas, while in jazz, it's the very core value of the genre. Here, improvisation unleashes innovation and spontaneous communication, crafting unique, fleeting moments of musical magic that leave an unforgettable experience on each performance. With every improvisational exchange, musicians tap into the power of the present, conjuring fresh sounds and sensations that resonate deeply with their audience.

Collective Participation

Collective participation is a foundational tradition of Black American music, encompassing storytelling, rhythm, emotive expressions, improvisation, call-

and-response, and spiritual invocation. In Black American music, collective participation manifests in various forms, from interactive exchanges between performers and audiences to congregational responses in the Black sermon tradition found in the Black church. This feature highlights the democratic nature of Black American music, encouraging individual expressions within a collective framework and underscoring the principle that everyone has value, a role, and a contribution. Collective participation makes Black American music a dynamic and powerful force, echoing its African origins' rhythms, melodies, and spirit beyond physical and temporal boundaries.

However, music education rarely explores the defining features of Black American music. This is systemically problematic on many levels. To address this issue, this book proposes an educational approach I have coined as an Organic Curriculum Practice. This perspective emphasizes the roots of African musical oral traditions. In education, to effectively teach jazz or any genre of Black American music, teachers must ensure artistic authenticity during experiential learning in music education. This educational approach supports an environment where music is not just a subject to be studied, but a lived experience, encouraging students to engage with music as a form of dialogue, creativity, and purpose. To achieve this objective, educators, musicologists, aficionados, and music lovers can draw upon their unique perspectives and expertise to develop innovative ideas. Provided are several activities that could assist you in the educational setting:

1. **Encourage Dialogue:** Utilize call-and-response to promote dialogue within the teaching and learning environment. Call-and-response rhythm exercises between the teacher and student or among the students could encourage active listening, spontaneous musical conversations, and collaborations reflecting Black American music.

2. **Explore the Social Functions of Music:** Assign projects that investigate the various roles of music in society, both historically and in contemporary contexts. Students can explore music to understand how it is used for storytelling, social critique, communal healing, and celebration across diverse cultures, drawing parallels between African cultural traditions and Black American music. Additionally, teachers can delve into the dynamic relationship between music and social-political movements, uncovering music as a tool for resistance, activism, and empowerment, and how it has reflected, influenced, and shaped human history.

3. **Integrate Storytelling into a Historical Context:** Introduce students to the stories behind the music that could involve the personal stories of jazz musicians and how their experiences shaped their music. Consider how jazz reflects and influences social and political movements. By understanding the context, students appreciate the music and its power as a form of expression and purpose.

4. **Cultivate Improvisation and Creativity:** Facilitate jam sessions and master classes with musical griots— revered musical knowledge and tradition keepers, allowing teachers to learn from music masters, honing skills, and deepening understanding of the music through hands-on experience and mentorship. When teachers encourage students to be themselves when improvising music, students can develop their voice within the musical environment.

5. **Promote Collective Participation:** Organize performances and attend musical events where students can participate as performers or simply be a part of a larger community experience, fostering a sense of belonging and connection to the music. Whether taking the stage or joining the audience, students can absorb the energy and passion of live music, develop a deeper appreciation for the art form, and become an integral part of the vibrant culture tapestry that Black American music represents.

6. **Support the Preservation and Transmission of Black American Music:** Teachers can take several steps to support preserving and transmitting Black American music heritage. First, teachers can document and archive the stories and experiences of Black American musicians, composers, and music industry professionals, ensuring their legacies are preserved for future generations. Second, teachers can also establish music education programs, workshops, and mentorship initiatives rooted in the history of Black American music, jazz theory, and performance practices, empowering intergenerational musicians. Third, teachers can promote and attend concerts, festivals, and events celebrating Black American music, supporting artists and cultural institutions dedicated to preserving and innovating within the genre. By taking these actions, teachers can help safeguard the rich cultural heritage of Black American music and ensure its continued vitality and influence.

7. **Incorporate Jazz Music into Educational Curricula and Programming:** Jazz music must seamlessly integrate into educational curricula and programming through various innovative approaches. For instance, educators can use jazz to teach music theory, history, and appreciation, highlighting its evolution and cultural significance. Interdisciplinary connections can be made by incorporating jazz across subject matter, such as literature and history. Moreover, jazz can assist with teaching improvisation, creativity, and collaboration skills, fostering critical thinking and problem-solving abilities. Schools can also invite jazz musicians for workshops, masterclasses, and performances, providing students hands-on experiences and inspiring future generations of jazz enthusiasts. By incorporating jazz into educational curricula and programming, teachers can enrich students' understanding of music, culture, and history while promoting creativity, diversity, and inclusivity.

By emphasizing the African roots, functionality, and communal traditions in the study of jazz and other genres of Black American music, educators can offer learners a rich and captivating experience, allowing students to acquire a deeper understanding of the cultural and historical significance of Black American Music, promoting mutuality and respect.

Dear readers, as we celebrate the rich diversity of Black American music, we also honor its African heritage. We recognize that Black American music, in all its forms, is not just entertainment but a vibrant, living testament to the resilience, creativity, and endurance of the African American spirit. It is a clarion call to remember and rejoice in the rhythm of life, a rhythm that echoes past struggles, present joys, and future hopes. In this recognition, we are both responsible and privileged to continue telling the story, keeping the music alive, and ensuring that the legacy of love and tradition passes doubtlessly through generations, inspiring, uplifting, and uniting us all.

CHAPTER ONE

Uncharted Territory

(1619-1865)

Upon the arrival of enslaved Africans to America in 1619, seeds were sown of African American folk genres such as field hollers, work songs, ring shouts, and Negro Spirituals. As enslaved Africans labored in the fields, they transformed their struggles into songs, marching to the rhythm of freedom with every step, fueled by their unwavering faith. Through coded language, enslaved Africans developed a powerful medium for resistance, enabling them to share knowledge, coordinate actions, and sustain their cultural heritage, ultimately nurturing a unifying spirit that drove their quest for freedom and self-determination. Meanwhile, the misguided notion that the enslaved people's singing was a sign of contentment and happiness was a pervasive and erroneous assumption held by many overseers, revealing a disconnect from the harsh realities of slavery.

Field hollers, an African American folk genre– also known as a field call marked by their intense emotional depth– exhibits similarities to the impassioned oratory of Black preachers, who skillfully rally their congregations with a call to spiritual awakening, evoking intense emotions of joy, inspiration, and fervent devotion. Field hollers were typically expressed as a personal and individual expression, contrasting with work songs' collective and communal nature.

On any given Sunday in the Black community, the preacher is a virtuosic storyteller, using the pulpit as an instrument to orchestrate a narrative of liberation. With lyrical language and melodic intonations, they conduct a symphony of freedom, accompanied by the percussive beats of drums, the soulful sounds of musical instruments, and the collective voices of the congregation, echoing in a chorus of amens, hallelujahs, and jubilant praise dancing.

Listen to the sorrow and unrest sentiments expressed in Mr. Lightnin Hopkin's version of the field Holler entitled "Go Down Old Hannah." This improvised masterwork is layered with coded language and words of resistance. In the lexicon of the enslaved, "Hannah" became a coded reference to the "Hot Sun" and the brutal forces of exploitation, which sought to suffocate their souls and snuff out their hope. There are several improvised verses to the song form. However, the chorus remains the same:

[Chorus]

Go down, go down, old Hannah
Woah Lord, don't you rise no more
Go down, go down, Hannah
Hannah, please don't rise no more
If I don't see your face, I don't believe
Poor Lightnin' gonna have to fool with that hoe

The brilliant rhyme schemes of the chorus provide a solid anchor for the spontaneous verse previously highlighted. The full song, composed of additional verses, was created in the heat of the moment through improvisation. Through the defiant voices of field hollers, the harmonious unity of work songs, and the soulful fervor of spirituals, African Americans transformed the attempts to suppress their communication into a sublime art form, weaving a rich tapestry of sound that chronicles their struggles, triumphs, and unyielding spirit.

While field hollers embrace a more fluid, improvisational approach, work songs anchor themselves in a steady, reliable rhythm. Both forms share a common thread of rhythmic ingenuity, demonstrating the versatility, adaptability, and fundamental unity that underlie the diverse landscape of folk music. Despite their rhythmic differences, both musical expressions share a common purpose to unite, inspire, and uplift the enslaved Africans in the field, serving as a powerful call to collective action and solidarity.

Another African American folk genre– spirituals– typically accompanied by a traditional dance known as the ring shout, has West African roots. The ring shout was a ceremonial dance where participants gathered in a circle and, with the start of the spiritual music, moved or shuffled around in a circular motion, often for hours. The dance started with slow, repetitive movements, gradually increasing in speed and energy until it reached a crescendo that triggered an ecstatic response from those participating. Jazz enthusiasts may experience a similar ecstatic response during the climactic moments of an improvisational solo, as the music reaches its peak intensity.

Negro Spirituals, carry a distinctive musical legacy tracing its roots back to the griots of West African Oral Traditions. However, many scholars are not in agreement concerning the origin of Negro Spirituals. According to music historian Eileen Southern, spirituals germinated during the 19th century (1800s). Other scholars, such as Dena Epstein and Samuel A. Floyd Jr., consider the spirituals to have started much earlier. The diverse sub-categories of Negro Spirituals– Sorrow songs, jubilee, and cult songs– may have different origins, shaped by the specific cultural, social, and religious contexts in which they evolved and serve distinct functional roles. These sub-category songs have existed and evolved since the 17th century.

The sorrow songs provided a powerful outlet for the enslaved to express their emotions and lament about the brutal realities of slave culture. Haunting songs like "Sometimes I Feel Like a Motherless Child" and "Nobody Knows the Trouble I've Seen" poignantly captured the anguish of oppression, with their resounding choruses conveying the crushing weight of mental suffering and the longing for freedom.

Jubilee spirituals, also known as camp meeting songs, such as "Every Time I Feel the Spirit" and "Rocky My Soul in the Bosom of Abraham," are characterized by their lively, upbeat rhythms and syncopated beats, conveying a sense of joy, celebration, and unbridled enthusiasm. These infectious songs, with energetic melodies and hand-clapping rhythms, evoke a sense of communal jubilation and triumphant freedom.

Cult spirituals utilized coded language and protest, exemplified in escape songs like "Still Away," "Swing Low Sweet Chariot," "Down by the Riverside," and "Wade in the Water." These songs served as a secret communication network, telegraphing escape strategies and tactics to evade detection by bloodhounds and slave catchers. By encoding their plans in song, enslaved individuals could covertly coordinate their escape routes and seek emancipation.

In simple terms, spirituals are heartfelt songs that acknowledge the mighty power of God, expressing gratitude for the blessings of health, life, and strength. Earl Stewart's *African American Music: An Introduction* defines spirituals as the earliest body of vernacular folk literature expressing the religious feeling of African Americans. I interpret this statement as illuminating the significance of spirituals as a vital part of African American cultural heritage, providing a window into the everyday language, imagery, and metaphors of spiritual messages.

Spirituals derive from the African technique of reshaping bits of pre-existing songs into new ones. The African cultural tradition of creative repurposing and transformation of existing materials likely inspired enslaved Africans to draw upon fragments of traditional hymns, African songs, Native American songs, and other pre-Civil War entertainment forms, synthesizing these diverse influences to create a fertile ground for a new musical genre to emerge. Improvisation succinctly mirrors the innovative process of reworking and recombining existing materials, ideas, designs, and concepts to create something entirely novel and unprecedented, venturing into uncharted territory. Undeniably, the early development of American Music inextricably links to improvisation and the innovative groundbreaking legacy of Negro Spirituals, which boldly explored new musical frontiers and shaped the nation's musical identity– Black American music– included.

The heritage of African American folk music has long demonstrated the capacity of Black American music to bring light to darkness and offer a balm of healing. The attributes of faith and hope inherent in these genres are vital for preserving musical authenticity and driving the quest for social justice and equality. Paul Robeson, internationally acclaimed performer, son of a runaway enslaved Black man and champion of the people, fashioned a very simple yet meaningful statement of responsibility: "An artist must elect to fight for freedom or slavery." Only by choosing freedom can an artist truly tap into their innovative potential and make a meaningful impact.

Exploring the Jazz Experience

The jazz experience– a cultural treasure– captures the essence of African American heritage. Individuality, relationships, respect, and a relentless pursuit of excellence fuel the spirit of jazz. Born from Black culture, jazz has evolved through a complex synthesis of African rhythms, Pentatonic scale harmony, and European harmony within a socio-political context. Jazz's improvisational nature mirrors Black Americans' spirit, transforming oppression into creativity. When listening to jazz, one must listen beyond the surface level, attending to the spaces between the notes and the intentional silences that shape each phrase, revealing the music's depth and rhythmic nuance. A key component of the *Jazz Experience* is mastering the art of silence and recognizing the power of pause as a vital part of the spirit of jazz. One must experience to know what it is. Understanding the Jazz Experience through the lens of its spiritual and ceremonial roots— spirituals and ring shouts—enriches our appreciation and celebration of Black American music. It deepens our understanding of its cultural significance. It reminds us that jazz music is not merely a musical genre but a vibrant, living history of dialogue between the past and present, continually evolving and resonating with each new generation

Quilted into the fabric of African American folk genres are the aesthetics of the functionality of jazz. Gregory Barz's Music in East Africa emphasizes the functions of traditional music for ritual and routine purposes, specifically in East Africa. Barz further indicates that musical performances are organized, maintained, planned, and used for funeral rites, therapeutic response, labor, timekeeping, communication, didactic response, educational purposes, and entertainment.

Music functions as a form of storytelling and education. For example, if a villager is a known thief or has committed a crime such as murder, music is used to alert the community and encourage individuals to change their ways. Thus, music is used indirectly as a non-threatening and socially acceptable method to address social issues and change in the village. Likewise, jazz music plays a vital role in American society. For example, in the 1960s, jazz music critiqued social issues and confronted socio-political issues and racism in the United States.

The 1960s were a particularly turbulent and violent era that, for Black Americans, resulted in a political, psychological, cultural, and historical reassessment and redefinition. For many newly emancipated Black people, a new definition of freedom was necessary to transcend the notion of simply being accommodated by a historically hostile or indifferent society. At this time, *Free Jazz,* known as Avant-Garde Nationalism, evolved into a new form of jazz that spoke to the era's issues. Stewart defines Avant-Garde Nationalism as "music reflecting political and cultural nationalism championed by radical Black artists and intellectuals of the period." Many of its aesthetic and stylistic attributes are best seen in these terms.

One prominent jazz musician and music pioneer in this era, John Coltrane, innovatively used the pentatonic scale, a hallmark of spirituals, his pioneering technique of rapid, cascading notes, dubbed "sheets of sound," as one of the most sublime artistic achievements in American Music. His vision: to represent a pinnacle of excellence in Black American cultural heritage, driven by a quest for peace, devotion, and spiritual awakening.

Walking in the footsteps of Black American music pioneers like John Coltrane is an encounter with the artistic soul of a people seeking freedom and liberation. Coltrane reached the souls of many listeners with his seminal work entitled *A Love Supreme*. This masterpiece consists of four sections that comprise an oral chant, a song composition recognizing the divine greatness of God, and an expression of gratitude. This album speaks to the spiritual impact of the jazz experience.

CHAPTER TWO

THE BLUES STORY

(1865-1885)

In the mid-19th century, antebellum South, Black people created Blues music in the United States. As explained in the previous chapter, African Americans in southern fields and plantations nurtured the roots of blues music, singing to cope with the relentless labor and harsh conditions through work songs, field hollers, ring shouts, Negro Spirituals, and other types of folksongs. As slavery ended and African Americans sought better opportunities in the urban areas, blues music was ultimately born as a post-slavery phenomenon where Black music performers could voice their everyday struggles, drawing on their inner convictions of faith and determination. Amiri Baraka, a noted Black American music scholar, asserted that Black people are blues people performing a Negro music in White America. Baraka's statement reflects Dr. King's commentary in his address to patrons of the 1964 Berlin Jazz Festival when he stated that the blues, "take the hardiest realities of life and put them into music, only to come out with some new hope or sense of triumph."

The first Great Migration from 1910 to 1940 significantly contributed to the dissemination of blues music, with cities like Chicago, Memphis, and St. Louis emerging as central hubs for blues musicians, each city developing its distinct style. Chicago Blues, for instance, emerged as a prominent genre characterized by the use of electric guitars, amplified harmonicas, and a more pronounced rhythm section with drums and bass guitar. This style, popularized by legends such as Muddy Waters and Howlin' Wolf, brought a raw, electrifying energy to their performances. This new urban environment influenced the themes of

Blues music, which evolved to reflect the complexities of city life, including issues of love, loss, and economic hardship.

Another subgenre of blues, Memphis Blues, emerged in Tennessee in contrast to Chicago Blues. Memphis Blues maintained a more acoustic sound, with artists such as B.B. King and Furry Lewis crafting guitar-driven melodies and poignant lyrics. The city's strategic location along the Mississippi River fostered a unique musical melting pot, where Delta Blues intermingled with gospel and jazz influences. This deliberate blending of electric and acoustic styles enriched and diversified blues music, contributing to its richness and diversity.

Building on this rich tapestry of diverse blues styles, we find a vibrant fusion of influences further enriching the genre's emotional depth and sonic landscape. This dynamic blend of traditions effortlessly gives rise to the St. Louis Blues style, encompassing a broader geographical range of influences. From the high-energy St. Louis jump blues– characterized by faster tempos, driving rhythms, and shouted vocals– to the Northeast Texas Boogie-Woogie blues dating back to the 1870s, which pioneered the first piano-exclusive branch of the Blues idiom, the city of St. Louis established the blues as one of the nation's most popular genres of music.

Throughout its regional variations, blues music retained its essence: a powerful means of expression and storytelling for Black people to voice their experiences and emotions in a world that often sought to silence them. The improvisational nature of blues enabled a dynamic, ever-evolving art form where musicians could weave their personal stories and perspectives into their songs, shaping a unique narrative with each performance.

The blues' impact resonated far beyond the Black community, paving the way for genres like jazz, gospel, rhythm & blues, and rock & roll. Artists such as Elvis Presley, The Rolling Stones, and Eric Clayton heavily drew from blues traditions, introducing the music to a broader global audience. However, it's crucial to acknowledge the cultural appropriation that often accompanies this crossover. While white musicians achieved fame and fortune from blues music, Black American musicians faced financial struggles and lacked recognition, highlighting the need for acknowledgement and equity. In the 21st century, a renewed effort has emerged to honor and preserve blues music's legacy. Active initiatives, including festivals, museums, and educational programs, aim to educate new generations about the roots of blues music and its impact on American society. These efforts actively work to recognize and celebrate the significant contributions of Black American musicians, ensuring their legacy is properly acknowledged and cherished.

As we honor the pioneers of blues music, their legacy continues to thrive, inspiring a new generation of artists who draw upon the rich cultural heritage and emotional depth that has defined the genre. This enduring spirit of blues music persists, captivating contemporary audiences with its authentic, timeless appeal, which speaks to listeners from diverse backgrounds. Through soulful guitar wails and heartfelt lyrics, blues testifies to the human spirit's capacity to overcome life's challenges. The genre embodies a paradoxical identity, simultaneously embracing joy, sorrow, struggle, and triumph in a shared space. Blues music provides insight into the Black experience and represents the pinnacle of consciousness in American art forms, skillfully capturing the intricate complexities of democracy. In his groundbreaking 1899 essay collection, *The Souls of Black Folk,* W.E.B. Du Bois eloquently explores the double consciousness of Black people, where two identities– Black and American– conflict. This phenomenon is characterized by the constant need to view oneself through the eyes of others. Blues music, born in the aftermath of the Emancipation Proclamation, captures this dichotomy and serves as a powerful microcosm of American Society, reflecting the Black experience in the United States.

For over 400 years, Black people in America have endured systemic oppression and exploitation, yet still await reparations for the atrocities inflicted upon them and their ancestors. The US government's broken promise of "40 acres and a mule" was a deliberate act of disenfranchisement, a heartbreaking betrayal that should not be underestimated. So, my beloved readers, I ask: what connects systemic oppression, broken promises, shattered expectations, and the experience of being both Black and American to Blues music? The answer is simple: everything. We are, indeed, a blues people.

Let's examine the features of Blues music. Blues embodies the complexities of Black American identity, voicing the struggles and triumphs of a community forged in the fire of oppression and creativity. Every note screams defiance, and every lyric tells a story of survival and pride. Like a phoenix, blues music is reborn from the flames of oppression. Its soulful melodies transform pain and hardship into influential, soul-stirring art. Shouts and expressive, bent tones of wailing narrate stories of hardship, loss, and injustice, while uplifting melodies and syncopated rhythms declare triumph, love, and liberation. This harmonious blend of light and dark fuels a steadfast community's unbreakable spirit and unwavering resolve. The duality of light and dark is not just a reflection of personal emotions but a commentary on the broader societal condition. Blues music, with its roots in the lived experiences of Black people, offers a unique perspective through which to understand American democracy. It reveals the contradictions and complexities of a nation that prides itself on freedom and equality while simultaneously perpetuating systemic inequality and oppression.

Blues music transcends melody. It's a historical chronicle, cultural expression, and portrait of the Black experience in America. Preserving stories and experiences keeps collective memories alive, refusing to let them fade. Through its raw honesty, blues challenges listeners to face harsh realities, past and present, while inspiring optimism for a brighter future. Blues music is a mirror and beacon, reflecting struggles and triumphs while illuminating a path forward. It honors the legacy of those who came before us, acknowledging the ongoing fight for justice and equality. Despite the pain, blues music reminds us of the insatiable joy and creativity that define our generation, affirming Black people's unbreakable spirit and unwavering determination.

And so, the blues continues to affirm us. Its indomitable spirit and unwavering determination inspire generations. This unbridled creativity and joy have nurtured a rich musical heritage, which blossomed in the Mississippi Delta, giving birth to the Delta blues tradition, a folk genre that would come to be known as Country Blues. Characterized by the soulful sounds of voice and harmonica or voice and guitar, Country Blues, often associated with the male voice, essence transcends gender, speaking to the universal human experience. However, the Country Blues genre is often synonymous with the southern male voice and guitar accompaniment. A rich legacy of Country Blues artists has unwittingly transformed the Mississippi Delta's folk blues into a globally acclaimed and enduring artistic treasure. These artists, often given nicknames, captivated audiences worldwide with their raw, passionate storytelling and unparalleled emotional depth.

The nickname "Sunny Boy" or "Sonny Boy" has been affectionately bestowed upon several unsung blues artists throughout history, with "Sonny Boy" being the preferred spelling among Delta blues enthusiasts. Carrying the legacy of this name signifies embodying a new era and propelling the blues tradition forward. One notable artist who exemplifies this legacy is bluesman Sonny Boy Williamson.

In African American communities, nicknames often emerge from a person's public persona, reflecting their character, charm, and ability to connect with others. The moniker "Sonny Boy" likely originated from Williamson's cool demeanor, charismatic stage presence, and special rapport with his audience. Among his peers, Williamson was the undisputed champion of the people.

Meanwhile, celebrated artist Robert Johnson, the King of the Delta Blues, sings about making life choices in his iconic song "Cross Road Blues." This powerful expression captures the human experience of facing literal and metaphorical crossroads and choosing the right path. Johnson's masterpiece represents the quintessential Delta blues sound, conveying urgency and desperation through his haunting voice and skilled guitar playing. The lyrics, "I went down to the crossroads, fell on my knees" (Johnson, 1936), reflect a poignant plea for guidance and salvation, resonating deeply with the struggles faced by Black Americans. Like many Blues songs, "Cross Road Blues" displays an impassioned spirit and a steadfast dedication to the quest for a better life.

The tradition of the Mississippi Delta Blues is rich with artists who, like Johnson, used their music to tell stories of hardship, promise, and redemption. These artists, often overlooked during their time, laid the groundwork for future musicians. Their contributions to blues music are invaluable, and their legacy inspires and influences artists worldwide.

In addition to Robert Johnson, there are countless other blues musicians whose work deserves recognition. Artists like Charley Patton, often referred to as the "Father of the Delta Blues," and Edward James "Son" House, Jr., known for his emotional intensity and powerful voice, played pivotal roles in shaping the sound and style of Delta Blues. These musicians, along with many others, transformed the tender, unfiltered emotion of Blues into a sophisticated and deeply moving art form.

Blues music's remarkable journey from the Mississippi Delta fields to the global stage showcases its colorful artistic appeal and universal relevance. This genre transcends borders, speaking directly to the human experience. Through their powerful music, Black American artists have amplified the voices of the voiceless and shed light on society's darkest corners, leaving an unforgettable footprint on our collective consciousness. As we continue to explore and appreciate Blues music, we honor the legacy of those who have come before us and recognize their impact on our culture and lives.

Years ago, I attended a jam session at the iconic Blue Note jazz club in New York City. The Blue Note is a mecca for tourists worldwide seeking to experience live Jazz, a quintessentially American music genre proficiently performed by talented American musicians throughout its history. The audiences at the Blue Note comprise both seasoned aficionados and newcomers to the Black American music experience. I recall in January 2001, on a winter morning, just after midnight, I met a tourist from Japan who was a patron of jazz history and a connoisseur of blues music. He had a deep understanding and a passionate interest in immersing himself in the live performance of Black American music, witnessing its vibrancy and energy firsthand.

On any given night, jazz legends would gather to jam, share stories, and learn from each other's improvisational techniques. On this early set, my mentor and fellow trumpeter, Ted Curson, organized a repertoire of jazz standards and jazz originals with avant-garde fire and flair. Despite the Japanese tourist's repeated request for a blues song, Ted remained focused on his artistic exploration. After each musical selection, the pleas for a blues song grew more urgent, "Blues, play Blues, please!!"

Finally, Ted Curson approached the microphone, looked directly at the tourist from Japan, and said to him, "Listen, I am the Blues." Ted Curson's astonishing response left the audience stunned and silent. However, his point was well-taken and truthful to the core. Blues music is larger than song form, harmonic progressions, or instrumentation. Although it also encompasses those things, Blues music is a way of life that embodies the evolution of a Black freedom movement in America.

For the Japanese patron, the request for a blues song may have been a desire to hear a particular musical form. Still, Ted Curson's response was an invitation to recognize that the blues is an intrinsic part of his and Black culture's collective identity. It's a reminder that the blues is not merely a series of notes and rhythms, but a narrative of human experience. Indeed, on that cold winter morning in New York City, American jazz trumpeter Master Theodore "Ted" Curson's proclamation, "I am the Blues," was a master class in Black American music. Decades later, I still remember those four words, which exemplified Black American music aesthetics and offered insight into the musical footprint of African American culture.

CHAPTER THREE

THE EVOLUTION OF BLUES

(1868-1917)

Blues music, a raw and emotionally charged genre, emerged from the rich cultural landscape of the Deep South. It served as a poignant soundtrack to the African American experience, capturing the struggle, resilience, and conviction of a community enduring slavery, segregation, and systemic oppression. Originating in the late 19th century during the Reconstruction era, blues distilled African Americans' pain and enduring aspirations through its distinct 12-bar structure, soulful melodies, and evocative storytelling.

Blues music provided a voice to the voiceless, reflecting the cries, whispers, and wails of those fighting for survival and dignity in a society determined to silence them. From the Mississippi Delta's rural expanses to America's bustling urban streets, the artistry of blues laid the groundwork for a century of Black American musical innovation. It influenced generations of artists and shaped the essence of American popular music.

The ratification of the 14th Amendment on July 9, 1868, marked a crucial turning point in the evolution of blues music, transforming it from an African American folk form into a distinct musical genre. The use of specific instruments by formerly enslaved Black people became a defining characteristic of the blues style. The banjo, an instrument with West African roots, played a significant role in the genre's development alongside the guitar and harmonica.

Throughout the early 1800s, African Americans used the banjo to express country folk blues from New England to Louisiana. By the early 1900s, the banjo was prominent in New Orleans-style jazz, showcasing its versatility and enduring influence on American music.

Blues music has evolved as a reflection of African American life and a powerful artistic expression, influenced a diverse range of musical genres and styles– primarily classified into Country Blues, Urban Blues, and Jazz Blues– and contributed to the cultural fabric of the United States.

> **Country Blues** is characterized by its solo vocal performances, often accompanied by instruments such as the guitar, banjo, or harmonica. This style typically features a bare and intimate sound, highlighting the artist's personal expression.

> **Urban Blues** involves a small ensemble setup, including instruments like bass, drums, percussion, guitar, banjo, and a solo vocalist. This style emerged as blues musicians migrated to cities, incorporating more sophisticated arrangements and a fuller sound.

> **Jazz Blues** is distinguished by a small combo featuring a rhythm section of bass, drums, or percussion, guitar, banjo, piano, and voice, occasionally complemented by a cornet. This style blends elements of jazz, offering greater harmonic complexity and opportunities for improvisation.

The artistic allure of the blues genre lies in its paradoxical blend of simplicity and sophistication. While Country and Urban Blues exhibit variations in instrumentation, they share a common AAB song form built around three primary chords: tonic, subdominant, and dominant. This straightforward structure belies the rich musical complexity and emotional depth that make blues a uniquely captivating art form.

The evolution of blues music, particularly within the Jazz Blues subgenre, has led to increased harmonic flexibility, longer song forms, and more opportunities for spontaneous improvisation. Unlike Country and Urban Blues, Jazz Blues occasionally deviates from the predictable AAB structure. A notable example is W.C. Handy's 1914 composition, "St. Louis Blues," which features an AABC structure, adding a 16-bar bridge section with elaborate harmonic variations. Jazz Blues often incorporates elements reminiscent of musical theatre, complete with decorative introductions, endings, codas, and refrains, showcasing a more complex and dynamic structure.

Jazz Blues ensembles exhibit distinct nuances, especially in the interplay between the vocal line and the cornet. The vocal line engages in a dynamic call-and-response dialogue with the cornet, creating a unique and intimate musical conversation. Occasionally, the cornet player plays in tandem with the vocal line, sometimes deviating slightly from the melody rather than following strict unison or harmony. A notable example of this interplay can be heard in "Pratt City Blues" by Bertha "Chippie" Hill and Louis "Satchmo" Armstrong.

While other blues styles and subgenre variants are beyond the three primary categories, the musicians ultimately define the genre. Their unique interpretations and expressions shape the blues and its diverse substyles. Pioneering artists born in the late 1800s, such as Blind Lemon Jefferson (Texas), Blind Willie Johnson (Texas), Blind Willie McTell (Georgia), and DeFord Bailey (Tennessee), significantly influenced the country blues genre with their innovative and impactful music. These legendary musicians and others made invaluable contributions to country blues' development and enduring legacy.

Country Blues

Music pioneer William Henry "Papa Charlie" Jackson (November 10, 1887 – May 7, 1938) was a Louisiana-born bluesman and songster who played banjo, guitar, and ukulele. Papa Charlie, who wrote and recorded songs that became blues standards, was the first musician to record himself-accompanied blues music. Blues historians have mainly overlooked Papa Charlie's significant contributions, giving him relatively little attention. Below are two verses from his notable composition, "I'm a Good Doing Papa."

[Verse 1]

I'm a good-doing papa, women just cry over me

I'm a good-doing papa, women just cry over me

When I leave a town, I leave'em full of misery

[Verse 2]

I'm a good-doing papa, don't mean nobody no harm

I'm a good-doing papa, don't mean nobody no harm

All I want's a good-lookin' woman, hanging on my arm

Delta Blues

The Delta Blues style, which emerged in the Mississippi Delta around 1880, is one of the earliest and most influential forms of blues music. It has spawned some legendary artists as a regional variant of Country Blues. Three native sons of the Mississippi Delta have made significant contributions to the genre, creating seminal works that have left a lasting impact. These principal artists are Son House, Charlie Patton, and Robert Johnson.

Son House (March 21, 1902 – October 19, 1988) mesmerized audiences with his emotive vocals and distinctive Delta slide guitar style, earning him legendary status in the blues world. His unique sound has inspired generations of musicians who emulate his technique. Below are two verses from his poignant composition, "Country Farm Blues," a lament that sheds light on the exploitative convict leasing programs instituted by Southern elites in the post-slavery era, aimed to force African American men to work without pay as prisoners.

[Verse 1]

Down South, when you do anything, that's wrong

Down South, when you do anything, that's wrong

Down South, when you do anything, that's wrong

They'll sure put you down on the country farm.

[Verse 2]

Put you down under a man they call "Captain Jack"

Put you down under a man they call "Captain Jack"

Put you down under a man they call "Captain Jack"

He' sure write his name up and down your back

Charlie Patton (April 1891 – April 28, 1934) tremendously impacted American music, inspiring a generation of Delta blues musicians. Musicologist Robert Palmer deemed him one of the most significant musicians of the 20th century. Patton's "High Sheriff Blues" is a powerful protest song addressing racial discrimination and the unjust treatment of African Americans. The lyrics reference Belzoni, the site of the tragic murder of Reverend George W. Lee, a pioneering civil rights advocate who fought for voting rights in the Mississippi Delta. Lee's registration to vote in 1955 made him a target of segregationist violence, leading to his assassination in "Bloody Belzoni" on May 7th, 1955. He is considered one of the early martyrs of the Civil Rights Movement. Below are two verses from Patton's poignant song.

[Verse 1]

Get in trouble at Belzoni

There ain't no use a screamin' and cryin'

Get in trouble in Belzoni

There ain't no use a screamin' and cryin'

Mr. Will will take you back

To Belzoni jail house flyin'

[Verse 2]

Le' me tell you folksies

How he treated me

Le' me tell you folksies

How he treated me

An' he put me in a cellar

Just as dark as it could be.

Robert Johnson (May 8, 1911 – August 16, 1938), one of the most influential musicians of the 20th century, was a masterful storyteller who captured the social, political, and psychological struggles faced by Black Americans. In his haunting song "Hellhound on My Trail," Johnson poignantly conveys the mental imprisonment of oppression, injustice, and the painful experience of being trapped in a society that presumes guilt. The composition alludes to the futile attempt to escape violent white lynching mobs, achieving physical liberation but not psychological freedom. Johnson's point is that African Americans could evade lynch mobs physically but never fully detach themselves from the omnipresent threat. This perspective was likely shaped by his childhood experiences listening to his stepfather's stories of escape from a lynching mob.

Johnson's stepfather, Charles Dodds, often shared the harrowing experience of his abrupt departure from Hazlehurst, Mississippi, where the threat of lynch mobs loomed large. With vivid recollections, he recounted his narrow escape, a desperate flight to Memphis, Tennessee, that left behind the promise of a thriving business- his prosperous Wick furniture store. The memories of that perilous time linger far beyond his generation, codifying a permanent footprint on the treacherous landscape of racial tension and fear that defined the Deep South during the Jim Crow era (1870s-1960s). While Charles Dodds escaped the threat of a physical lynching, his stepson Robert Johnson wrestled with the psychological torment and fear that are central to his haunting musical legacy. Robert Johnson's "Hellhound on My Trail" is a powerful allegory for lynching, referencing the bloodhounds used to track fugitives, a practice dating back to slavery.

[Verse 1]

Got to keep movin', I got to keep movin'

Blues fallen' down like hail, blues fallin'

Down like hail, Hmm-mmm, blues fallin',

Down like hail, blues fallin' down like hail

And the days keeps on worryin' me

There's a hellhound on my trail

[Verse 2]

You sprinkled hot foot powder, hmm

All around my door

You sprinkled hot foot powder, hmm

All around your daddy's door, hmm-hmm

It keeps me with ramblin' mind, rider every

Old place I go, every old place I go

These musical pioneers of blues music paved the way for the liberation and celebration of Black American music, issuing a powerful call to freedom. Meanwhile, a new artistic visionary emerged: Charles "Buddy" Bolden, often regarded as the father of jazz. Bolden's innovative spirit crafted a new frontier in Black American music, laying the blueprint for the evolution of African American music at the turn of the 20th century. His collective improvisation concept and his ensemble's unique sound anticipated the joyful, celebratory tones that would later redefine blues music. Buddy Bolden's ensemble was the first to lay the anatomical foundation for the future jazz bands that followed.

Charles Joseph "Buddy" Bolden

Charles "Buddy" Bolden (September 6, 1877 – November 4, 1931), affectionately known as King Bolden, was a pioneering cornetist from New Orleans, where he performed from 1900 to 1907. Despite the severe oppression and denial of basic human rights faced by Black Americans during the rise of the

Jim Crow era, Buddy Bolden's band poignantly captured the sorrows and joys of their experiences. In the face of bitter adversity, he crafted melodies that embodied grief and joy, providing a way to cope with his environment and his many challenges. Paradoxically, the music Bolden created, framed by the societal challenges of his time, laid the footing for what many now regard as America's classical music: jazz.

King Bolden's ensemble was the prototype for New Orleans-style jazz, showcasing a unique blend of musical characteristics. These included collective improvisation, rhythmic concepts of ragtime, ceremonial feel of marching band music, spiritual fervor of Black church hymns, guttural moans inspired by the Blues, and various elements of African vocal traditions. Bolden's rich musical legacy and innovative blending of diverse influences helped pattern an American identity imbued with ingenuity and triumph. His music symbolizes strength and joy, offering African Americans new possibilities and pride in facing adversity.

Bolden's most significant contribution to American music is encapsulated in the sound of jazz as an American music art form. Today, jazz is now recognized worldwide as America's classical music. Despite Bolden's struggles and enigmatic life, Bolden's cornet playing sparked a cultural revolution during the classic jazz era, infusing an artistic freedom movement in the United States with meaning and purpose. His trumpet work at the turn of the 20th century set the standard for future jazz masters, and his band's leadership showcased his personality's emotional depth and power. Without Buddy Bolden, there would be no Louis Armstrong. When you hear Louis Armstrong, you hear Buddy Bolden.

Although no recordings of Bolden's music exist, some essayists and musicologists suggest that his legend might exceed his actual genius. His ability to herald a new era cemented his celebrity status. Interestingly, his existence was part of a larger freedom movement long before his birth. Bolden's trumpet sound is rooted in his ancestral DNA, tracing back to the African Diaspora's spirit and manifesting in Congo Square's communal celebrations. His legacy was symbolically authenticated in the 2019 film *Bolden*, directed by Dan Pritzker, featuring an original soundtrack written by Wynton Marsalis. Notably, I contributed to the movie as a trumpet coach for the Bolden character, portrayed by Gary Carr.

As the Father of Jazz, Bolden's blues-inspired sounds continue to evolve and resonate throughout American music history. His work testifies to the transformative power of turning adversity into art with remarkable skill and creativity, which continues to inspire and influence American music.

CHAPTER FOUR

The King of Ragtime

(1890-1917)

A notable genre born from African American musical traditions that revolutionized American music in the late 19th and early 20th centuries is Ragtime. This piano style of music originated in Sedalia, Missouri, shortly after the Civil War, and went on to influence the course of American music. Ragtime music is characterized by syncopated rhythms with accented notes played off the beat, creating a lively, happy feel. Scott Joplin, known as the "King of Ragtime," was a visionary composer and pianist who elevated the genre to an art form, breaking racial barriers and transcending cultural boundaries. He created one of the most recognizable syncopated rhythms and happy piano lines of the 20th century with his song "The Entertainer." This piece evokes various associations– a Western saloon, a grand escapade, an ice cream truck, and a silent movie soundtrack– yet its historical context is often forgotten. Born in 1868, Joplin was a visionary artist who achieved greatness despite facing racism and poverty. His music continues to influence America's social and musical structures a century after his death. Joplin's 1899 song, "Maple Leaf Rag," was the first instrumental piece to sell over 1 million copies during the composer's lifetime, commercially achieving broad appeal and mass consumption, thereby ushering in the ragtime era and defining America's first popular music craze.

To appreciate the significance of ragtime, it's essential to understand its predecessors. Before Scott Joplin's rise to fame, John Philip Sousa was one of America's most popular songwriters. As a military band leader, Sousa composed marches designed for walking, with his most famous work being *Stars and*

Stripes Forever. These influential marches typically featured 2/4 or 4/4 time with an expected emphasis on down beats. In contrast, Black music, designed for dance, employs a different approach. Syncopation, which involves accenting unexpected beats or missing expected ones, is fundamental to various Black American music genres. The syncopation technique that defines Black music was introduced to American popular music through the infectious rhythms of ragtime. Scott Joplin's iconic "Maple Leaf Rag" demonstrates this, its distinctive, off-kilter vibe evoking the confident strut of a silent film star. The rise of silent films in the late 19th century coincided with the golden age of ragtime, and the two art forms became inextricably linked. In the 21st century, American popular music remains rooted in the same foundational values established during this era. These values can be condensed into five primary pillars: 1) commercial accessibility, 2) the novelty of technology, 3) the ability to transcend language and cultural barriers, 4) visual staging, and 5) capitalist appropriation. Later in this chapter, we'll look at the artistic values embedded in Scott Joplin's masterwork, "Maple Leaf Rag," and further explore Scott Joplin's perennial significance.

Minstrel music, a complex and problematic genre, significantly influenced the development of ragtime. Surfacing in the American South in the early 1800s, minstrelsy was a type of staged entertainment that featured white performers in blackface, perpetuating demeaning stereotypes and appropriating Black American music and culture for the financial gain of white audiences. Despite the painful history of exploitation and racism, minstrel shows were incredibly popular, generating enormous wealth for their creators. However, it's essential to acknowledge this context to understand the broader legacy of American music and the psychological impact on the concept of Black American popular music. Interestingly, some Black artists navigated this treacherous environment to launch their careers, and one notable example is the cakewalk. This dance originated in Black communities during the pre-Civil War era. Known initially as the *prize walk,* this dance comprises a distinctive 2/4 march time and syncopated polyrhythm, known as hemiola. The cakewalk's popularity in minstrel shows has stirred debate about its origins, with some arguing it satirized white dances. Regardless, the cakewalk remains an integral part of American music history, reflecting the complex and often fraught relationship between Black culture and white appropriation.

Polyrhythms, such as the three-over-two patterns in Joplin's "Maple Leaf Rag," are rooted in sub-Saharan African music traditions. These polyrhythms evolved into the habanera and clave rhythm conception in Afro-Cuban music, prominently featured in African Diaspora music, including Haitian drumming, Brazilian music, and New Orleans second-line music. The Texas hambone rhythm, a body percussion technique developed by enslaved Africans in North America, emerged due to the 17th century ban on drumming to prevent slave revolts. This technique involved creating rhythms on various body parts, incorporating influences from the habanera and clave rhythms, and rhythmic patterns derived from African languages. From 1890 to 1917, the ragtime era flourished as musicians embraced and developed these rhythms, generating widespread support.

Ragtime musicians honed their craft in saloons, brothels, bars, and other venues along the Mississippi and Missouri rivers in the late 19th century. New Orleans-born ragtime legend Tony Jackson thrived in Storyville's red-light district, known for risqué activity but a space for Black jazz musicians to develop their craft, influencing younger players like Jelly Roll Morton, Clarence Williams, and Steve Lewis. Other notable itinerant pianists who contributed to ragtime's musical footprint include Charles Hunter, Thomas Turpin, Louis Chauvin, and Charles L. Jones. These musicians, hailing from across the country, mastered the new frenzy of ragged/syncopated rhythms and crafted march time, giving birth to African American culture's first popular music. Some of the first published ragtime songs, such as Ernest Hogan's 1895 piece, "La Pas Ma La," were also formidable minstrel show performances.

Ernest Hogan (1865-1909)

Hailing from Bowling Green, Kentucky, Ernest Hogan broke new ground as the first Black entertainer to produce and star in a Broadway show, "The Oyster Man," in 1907. In 1895, Hogan composed one of the earliest rags, "La Pas Ma La," which drew inspiration from the Pasmala dance. With its distinctive forward strut and three steps back, this dance has evolved into various celebratory dances within the African American community. Today, these dances are frequently seen at weddings, family reunions, parties, conferences, and other special gatherings, highlighting Hogan's lasting impact on African American culture. The chorus of the song captures its essence:

[Chorus]

Hand upon yo' head, let your mind roll back,

Back, back, back and look at the stars

Stand up rightly, dance it brightly

That's the Pas Ma La.

Hogan's next major song, "All Coons Look Alike to Me," was a commercial success, selling over a million copies. However, the song's use of a racial slur in its title and lyrics caused significant outrage among African Americans. This success led to a trend of coon songs that reinforced racist stereotypes, casting a shadow over Hogan's legacy as a ragtime pioneer. Despite this controversy, Hogan's compositions were among the first ragtime pieces published and the first to feature the term "rag" in their sheet music. Tom Fletcher, a fellow Black American musician, credited Hogan as the first to notate the unique rhythm that non-reading musicians were playing. In 1900, semi-finalists at the World Competition's ragtime championship in New York performed Hogan's "All Coons Look Alike to Me" to showcase their talents.

Ben Harney (1872-1938)

Another notable figure in ragtime music was Benjamin Robertson Harney. As some sources suggest, Ben Harney, who originated from Louisville, Kentucky, or possibly Nashville, Tennessee, played a remarkable role in popularizing ragtime music. Early in his career, Harney claimed to have invented ragtime, a statement that drew criticism for ignoring the genre's Black origins. Despite Scott Joplin's association with ragtime, the New York Times noted in 1924 that Harney might have done more to popularize the genre than anyone else. The Library of Congress acknowledges Harney's 1895 composition, *You've Been a Good Old Wagon but You Done Broke Down,* as the first published ragtime song. Originally written for piano and voice, it became the first ragtime hit to reach mainstream audiences. While not a standard hard-core ragtime piece due to its 16-bar (AABB) song structure, Harney's later work, *Cakewalk in the Sky,* published by M. Witmark & Sons in New York in 1898, showcased key ragtime features in solo piano, duple time, and four melodic sections/themes.

Much like the blues, ragtime music embraces diverse styles and expressions. From this diversity, a trailblazer who would elevate the genre to unprecedented heights resurfaced.

Scott Joplin (1868- 1917)

Scott Joplin's arrival on the scene marked a turning point, and in 1899, he published two piano scores that revolutionized ragtime: "Maple Leaf Rag" and "Original Rag." These seminal works codified ragtime, setting a new standard for the genre. Characteristically, Joplin's compositions featured frequent modulations, a technique that involves shifting from one tonal center to another within a song. In ragtime, this meant moving between distinct key centers, creating a rich harmonic palate. Joplin's structural innovation consisted of four sections following an AABBACCDD pattern, with the C-section typically featuring a precise modulation, often in the form of a Key change. For instance, in "The Entertainer," the C-section of the composition modulates to the key of F major, while the rest of the song remains in the key of C major.

Developing ragtime music further, Scott Joplin's compositions showcased another crucial element: tempo. Contrary to popular associations with fast piano playing, ragtime was designed for moderate-paced playing, according to Joplin. He even annotated "Not Fast" on the piano score of "The Entertainer." When played at a slower tempo, the song unfolds like a narrative, with dramatic tension and shifts in key and volume. Ragtime music, "The Entertainer" and "Maple Leaf Rag" became genre staples, inspiring countless imitations. However, Joplin's ambitions extended beyond popular music.

Scott Joplin sought to elevate Black American musicians as serious songwriters and composers. To achieve this, he wrote an opera, *Treemonisha*, drawing inspiration from African American folktales and blending ragtime with classical and operatic traditions. The opera's "A Real Slow Drag" finale highlights this fusion. Moreover, *Treemonisha* conveys a vital social message, advocating for civil rights and education to advance racial equality and justice in America. Through his opera, *Treemonisha*, Joplin sought to create a genuinely original Black art form, and in its title character, he crafted a powerful symbol of empowerment. The Treemonisha character is a young, free Black woman who uses education to empower her community and resist exploitation. This forward-thinking story is paired with remarkable music, showcasing Joplin's innovative spirit. However, Joplin's vision was never fully realized. Despite his efforts, Joplin couldn't find a publisher for his radical opera and self-published it in 1915. Unfortunately, he only managed to stage a miniature, scaled-down version in the Harlem rehearsal hall, far from his grandiose vision. This disappointment marked the beginning of the end of the ragtime era, a poignant conclusion to Joplin's pioneering journey. In 1917, Scott Joplin's struggles finally caught up to him, and he descended into dementia and died in a psychiatric hospital, a tragic end to a life marked by innovation and perseverance. Despite his contributions to American music, Joplin was laid to rest in an unmarked grave, a distressing record of his neglect in his final years. As the legacy of Scott Joplin's ragtime era ended, a new chapter in American music was unfolding, and the city that would come to define it was about to take center stage. While the Great Migration brought musicians from the South, Midwest, and other parts of the country to New York City during the Harlem Renaissance of the 1920s, a talented artist was already launching a shift from ragtime to the piano style known as stride.

Thomas Wright "Fats" Waller (1904-1943)

A prolific composer, he exemplified brilliance and humor in his music, as seen in his iconic musical, *Ain't Misbehavin,* represents an ideal prototype of the stride piano movement. His work embodied a paradox, reflecting the African American experience during the era of Jim Crow– a mix of joy, brilliance, and suffering under discrimination and oppression. Yet, through his music, Waller delivered a triumphant spirit of love. In the stage production, *Ain't Misbehavin,* one of Waller's most unforgettable compositions is "What Did I Do To Be So Black and Blue," an early attempt to address racism openly. This protest song showcases Waller's ability to convey the hardships faced by Blacks in a racist society, highlighting the conflict between feelings and societal expectations. Waller's talent was multifaceted, as seen in "A Handful of Keys," which showcases his stride piano virtuosity.

Thomas "Blind Tom" Greene Wiggins (1849-1908)

In celebration of piano virtuosity, it's essential to acknowledge the remarkable story of Thomas Wiggins, aka "Blind Tom," an African American blind and autistic servant and musical prodigy. Born into slavery near Columbus, Georgia, Wiggins demonstrated extraordinary talent from an early age, playing tunes, he had only heard by age four. Despite his limited vocabulary of barely a hundred words, he composed dozens of original pieces and could perform hundreds more from memory. In 1862, at 12 years old, Wiggins listened intently to a description of the Battle of Manassas. He subsequently composed his famous masterpiece, which he performed at concerts and war effort fundraising events without compensation, while his owners accumulated wealth from these performances. Due to his popularity, Wiggins became one of the most renowned American performers, solidifying his position as a musical icon from the mid-to-late 19th century to the present.

Building on the foundations laid by Blind Tom Wiggins, the next generation of piano masters– Willie "The Lion" Smith, Art Tatum, Eubie Blake, James P. Johnson, Lucky Roberts, and Jelly Roll Morton– propelled the evolution of ragtime into stride piano forward, paving the way for a new chapter in Scott Joplin's story to unfold.

Musical Coda

In 1970, musician and musicologist Joshua Rifkin rediscovered Joplin's music scores. They released a recording titled "Scott Joplin: *Piano Rags"* that sparked a ragtime revival, and three years later, Joplin's songs, including "The Entertainer," were featured prominently in George Roy Hill's Oscar-winning film, *The Sting.* Scott Joplin's music once again captured the hearts of American pop culture. Amidst this resurgence, Joplin's forgotten opera "Treemonisha" was unearthed. In 1972, sixty-one years after it was written, the opera received its world premiere by the Atlanta Symphony Orchestra under Robert Shaw. In 1976, Joplin posthumously received a Pulitzer Prize for *Treemonisha,* finally recognizing this masterpiece. The world was ready to embrace the late Joplin and celebrate his brilliant, forward-thinking artistry. In 1974, after lying unmarked for half a century, Scott Joplin's grave finally received a well-deserved marker.

Ragtime's impact on American society and culture influenced the development of jazz, blues, and popular music while also reflecting the struggles and aspirations of African Americans during the Reconstruction era (1865-1817). Through its unique blend of classical and folk elements, ragtime embodies the spirit of American ingenuity and creativity, cementing its place as a beloved and enduring part of our musical heritage.

CHAPTER FIVE

THE CLASSIC JAZZ ERA: THE SUNBURST OF

BLACK AMERICAN CULTURE

(1900-1930)

The classic jazz era, spanning 1900 to 1930, consists of two distinct phases: New Orleans style jazz (1900-1917) and Chicago-style jazz (1917-1930), with the latter defining the second phase. The first phase, New Orleans style jazz, emerged in the city's vibrant neighborhoods of New Orleans, Louisiana, where African American musicians drew upon their cultural heritage to create a distinctive sound. This colorful cultural melting pot harmoniously blended diverse influences while preserving their identities. The city's renowned Creole heritage—a rich fusion of Native American, French, West African, and Spanish cultures—sets the stage for a unique musical experience.

New Orleans was home to a vast range of celebrated music traditions, including the blues, African American spirituals, gospel hymns, John Philip Sousa's marching band legacy, syncopated brass bands, European classical music, ragtime, popular songs, minstrelsy, and African music traditions. This convergence of styles in the New World gave birth to a dynamic and influential symbol of creativity and ingenuity. As the first steamboats emerged on the Mississippi River, New Orleans became one of the world's largest ports, handling trade from the Mississippi River Valley, the Eastern Seaboard, Europe, the Caribbean, and Latin America. This cultural vessel ultimately gave rise to a distinctive form of African American music that embodied various traditions and serendipitously created a new musical expression of freedom—Jazz.

Congo Square, established in 1817 and now known as Louis Armstrong Park, was more than just an open field- it was a vital space for resistance and cultural preservation. On Sundays, their only day off, enslaved Africans in New Orleans would gather to play drums, string instruments, sing, dance, and speak their native languages. The Sunday afternoon gatherings featured circular dance movements and clusters of people, echoing the ritual ceremonies of Africa and the celebrated dance known as the ring shout. Congo Square was also a hub for the concept of Ngoma, a West and East African tradition that connected music and dance, bringing vibrant religious rituals, social gatherings, and healing practices to the New World. This cultural melting pot allowed musicians to merge their traditions, reshaping existing songs into new ones. The tradition thrived until around 1885, coinciding with the emergence of the first jazz bands in New Orleans. As a pivotal link in the history of Black music culture in the United States, Congo Square in New Orleans, Louisiana, is a crucial part of American history and a national landmark.

Louis Armstrong Carnegie Hall 1947

Although the public gatherings ceased, the ring shout tradition became integral to the second line musical culture. This tradition, brought by enslaved Africans, became a ritual for African Americans, particularly in processions like funerals. Scholars note the similarities between the West African ring shout and the second line tradition, including the exaggerated, stylistic strutting steps. Once banned for being deemed threatening, these dances resurfaced in the second line culture, celebrating individual freedom.

The second line culture is a colorful tradition in New Orleans parades, organized by social aid and pleasure clubs. These clubs and benevolent societies invited communal participation, encouraging everyone to join the procession. The parade's central section, or "mainline," features grand marshals, church and club members, and a brass band. In contrast, the "second line" refers to the enthusiastic followers who trail behind the band, reveling in the music, dance, and community spirit. With handkerchiefs and parasols in hand, they embody the joy and collective energy of the occasion.

This quintessential New Orleans tradition is deeply rooted in African American culture, making it one of the most enduring and authentic Black American retentions in the United States. The music played at these events—blues and spirituals like "When the Saints Go Marching In"— characterized individual expression and collective cohesion. As the music becomes more upbeat, the second line participation grows, fostering a sense of community and cultural connection. This transplanted African ritual remains deeply ingrained in the collective memory of New Orleans' Black community and the early jazz pioneers, serving as a testament to the power of cultural resilience and creativity.

As highlighted earlier, Charles Bolden– recognized as "King Bolden" or "Buddy Bolden"– a cornetist and one of the earliest jazz pioneers, revolutionized music by assimilating diverse influences into his unique improvisational approach. Bolden's innovative spirit also led to the development of the "Big Four," a key rhythmic innovation that transformed the marching band beat. As Wynton

Marsalis explains, this syncopated bass drum pattern "deviated from the standard on-the-beat march pattern, introducing more room for individual improvisation." The "Big Four" pattern in the second half of the fourth beat is commonly known as the hambone rhythm, rooted in sub-Saharan African music traditions. Bolden's interpretive and ground-breaking work inspired a generation of jazz pioneers, who built upon his creativity and newfound freedom in jazz music.

Early New Orleans jazz was considered immoral music as it was associated with the red-light district previously highlighted. Even publications as prestigious as The New York Times wrote anti-jazz articles that shared this sentiment, but these efforts failed to halt the genre's rising popularity. In 1917, the military closed the Storyville red-light district, but by then, jazz had already caught the attention of talented young musicians like Jelly Roll Morton, Kid Ory, Sidney Bechet, Joseph "King" Oliver, and his protégé, Louis Armstrong.

Sidney Bechet, 1947 at Jimmy Ryan's (Club) NYC

Born in the "back of town," Armstrong would arguably become the most incredible sensation in American music history. The proliferation of talented New Orleans musicians made jazz one of the most innovative and original African American cultural art forms. Notably, the first jazz recording made by the Original Dixieland Jazz Band, an all-white band from New Orleans in 1917, falsely claimed to be the inventors of jazz while introducing a watered-down version of the genre to a larger American audience. However, a group of Black soldiers would take jazz to an international audience.

During World War I, James Reese Europe, a gifted musician and composer from Mobile, Alabama, led a band as the Harlem Hellfighters 369th infantry regiment, who played jazz throughout Europe during World War 1. After the war, the band continued to spread jazz globally. With pioneers like Charles "Buddy" Bolden, Joseph "King" Oliver, Fletcher Henderson, Louis Armstrong, and Duke Ellington, jazz became incredibly popular, earning in the 1920s the nickname "The Jazz Age." Jazz evolved into the first original, sophisticated instrumental music in American history from its humble and controversial origins. Indeed, the Jazz Age, a manifestation of the classic jazz era, created a celebration of diverse performance traditions in Black American music and nurtured those musical giants whose footsteps we follow.

The Second Phase (1917-1930) of the classic jazz era witnessed an explosion of radical musical innovation, converging diverse artistic expressions in Black American music. Chicago was abuzz with the emergence of gospel music, its roots digging deep into African American folk traditions, and Chicago-style jazz. Musicologists agree on this timeline, noting that Chicago-style jazz emerged after the closure of Storyville in 1917. This shift triggered the migration and relocation to the north. Many musicians, including trumpeter King Oliver, left New Orleans in 1918 after World War I and headed to Chicago for better opportunities.

Chicago was a kettle where diverse musical styles merged, igniting a cultural renaissance. Musically, Chicago-style jazz was a cousin of New Orleans-style jazz, sharing a similar DNA but with distinct differences. One notable distinction was instrumentation. Chicago jazz ensembles often used the guitar instead of the banjo, traded tubas for upright basses, and added the velvety voice of tenor saxophones. The piano also became a staple, injecting tension and harmonic complexity into the music. As the city reverberated with a faster, more urban rhythm, solos took center stage, showcasing individual proficiency. The musicians played with greater finesse, driven by the city's unrelenting pace.

Chicago, a bustling industrial hub in the 1920s, drew young workers from far and wide, including African Americans fleeing southern states for better opportunities. A vibrant cultural design unfolded as New Orleans and Chicago musicians merged their styles.

Thomas A. Dorsey, the father of Black gospel music, blazed a new path, crafting over 3,000 compositions, including the iconic "Take My Hand, Precious Lord." His 50-year tenure as music director at Pilgrim Baptist Church in Chicago, Illinois, produced the first widely-known gospel choir.

Dorsey mentored a talented generation of gospel singers, including Sallie Martin, Mahalia Jackson, Roberta Martin, and a young James Cleveland. However, his initial fame emerged in the 1920s as a leading figure in urban blues, alongside outstanding women artists like Ma Rainey, known as the "Mother of the Blues." Meanwhile, Jelly Roll Morton, an ingenious ragtime pianist and composer, transformed the genre by fusing it with jazz, further fueling this remarkable surge in African American creativity.

Amidst the vibrant mural of Black American music in the Classic Jazz era, Joseph "King" Oliver's band shone brightest in Chicago. As a trumpeter, bandleader, and composer from New Orleans, Oliver mentored the legendary Louis Armstrong and introduced the use of brass mutes in jazz. This novelty birthed a new language in jazz, rooted in African vocality, with the plunger mute's emotive shouts, bends, and growls enriching the music's lyricism and depth.

In 1920, Oliver formed his Creole Jazz Band, featuring one of the first women in jazz, pianist-composer Lil Hardin, as an original member. Two years later, he summoned Armstrong, his protégé, to join the band as second cornetist, showcasing his enterprising leadership. In 1923, the band recorded 42 numbers, including Oliver's iconic "Dippermouth Blues," whose plunger mute solo became a benchmark for future generations. "Dippermouth Blues" epitomizes the dynamic fusion of blues and ragtime in early jazz. This measured composition blends ragtime's bright, multi-thematic spirit with the soulful, 12-bar blues core, creating a unique soundscape showcasing the genre's eclectic roots. This 1923 recording represents Armstrong and Oliver's earliest recordings in their illustrious career.

Dippermouth Blues was composed by King Oliver & Louis Armstrong. Recorded by Gennett records in 4/1923 & Okeh records on 6/1923. Personnel:

- Joe "King" Oliver – leader, First Cornet (muted solo)

- Louis Armstrong – Second Cornet

- Honore Dutrey – Trombone

- Johnny Dodds – Clarinet

- Lil Hardin – Piano

- Bill Johnson – Banjo

- Baby Dodds – Drums

Let's examine the musical timetable of "Dippermouth Blues" and uncover how this masterpiece unfolds with original flair. As we explore its structure, we'll hear and discover how the notes seem to dance, weaving a rich tapestry of sound that showcases King Oliver's creative genius.

Intro 0:00 - Oliver and Armstrong play a short duet opener (two cornets presenting an element of surprise).

A-0:06 - Band begins with a New Orleans sound: the 1st chorus ignites with the ensemble's collective improvisation. 0:21- Clarinetist Johnny Dodds improvises a counter melody for twelve measures. Dodds' improvised counter melody is in tandem with the central melodic theme played by Oliver's lead cornet.

A1- 0:37 - Clarinet continues with a featured improvised counter melody for 12 measures. In contrast to the ensemble's stop time rhythmic pattern for ten 10 measures. The stop time rhythmic patterns have accents on beats 123; subsequently followed by a two-measure turnaround melodic phrase. 0:53- The clarinet feature continues to develop thematic ideas. The ensemble continues with stop-time rhythmic patterns.

A2- 1:10 - Louis Armstrong plays the solo lead part carrying the melody in the foreground. The ensemble plays similarly to the previous chorus with added trombone texture/substance.

A3-1:26 - Oliver's legendary innovative plunger mute solo invoking attributes of African vocality (i.e., bent notes, wah-wah effects, blues delivery created with sound). Utilization of notes connected to the upper structural #9 harmonic approach throughout his first chorus. Oliver's rhythmic feel (i.e., the big four conception with accents placed in the second half of beat four) intensifies his sound's tinge. 1:42 - Oliver's solo work continues introducing a new upper tessitura pitch in his improvisational approach. Brilliant use of theme and variation, three-note motifs, and call-and-response patterns. 1:58- Oliver's solo work intensifies with a new upper tessitura pitch expansion. 2:12- The ensemble vocal shout declares the following lyric: *Oh play that thing!!!*

A4 -2:14 - Oliver & Armstrong lead the ensemble for a final out chorus of twelve (12) measures, adding a two (2) measure tag ending.

King Oliver's innovative trumpet playing, storytelling imagination, and resourceful use of everyday objects like the toilet and sink plunger left an unforgettable memory on the classic Jazz era. His pioneering work in New Orleans and subsequent recordings with Gennett and Okeh Records in Chicago helped shape a new sound. Oliver's distinctive "wah-wah" mute sounds also inspired Patrick T. Harmon's interest in creating a mute that captured the essence of Black jazz bands, leading to the development of a 1925 trumpet and trombone Harmon mute that echoed this unique sound.

"The King Oliver Creole Jazz Band," featuring Louis Armstrong and Lil Hardin Armstrong (husband and wife), wielded immense influence over generations of musicians. However, the group's premature disbandment in September 1924 stemmed from Armstrong's departure to join Fletcher Henderson's Orchestra in New York City.

Fletcher Henderson, a visionary pianist, bandleader, arranger, and composer, helmed the most elite ensemble in New York, showcasing his mastery at the esteemed Roseland Ballroom. His 10-year residency featured a dream team of musicians, including saxophone virtuoso Coleman Hawkins, arranger extraordinaire Don Redman, alto sax pioneer Benny Carter, and the incomparable Louis Armstrong, alongside a constellation of future icons who helped shape the Harlem Renaissance. Henderson and Duke Ellington stand as titans in jazz history, but Armstrong would ascend to unparalleled heights, becoming the most resounding sensation in American music.

Louis Armstrong (August 4, 1901 – July 6, 1971) was a trailblazing trumpeter, vocalist, actor, and political activist, affectionately known as Pop, Satchmo, Dippermouth, and Satchel Mouth. He was a true pioneer in Black American music, embodying the spirit of Phyllis Wheatley, Harriet Tubman, and Frederick Douglass. Armstrong's statesmanship and revolutionary contributions in the 1920s transformed the music scene. He innovatively used his voice as an instrument, improvising wordless sounds in scat singing, which conveyed his emotions with unparalleled depth.

In 1925, Armstrong returned to Chicago from New York to form his first recording jazz band, Louis Armstrong and His Hot Five, followed by Louis Armstrong and His Hot Seven. The personnel included Kid Ory (trombone), Johnny Dodds (clarinet), Johnny St. Cyr (banjo), Pete Biggs (tuba), and John Thomas (trombone), who replaced Kid Ory. During a prolific period, they produced twenty-four recordings, with the timeless classic "West End Blues" standing as a tribute to Armstrong's impactful legacy.

Louis Armstrong's Hot Five produced twenty-four recordings over a twenty-four-month period. I believe the most seminal piece from this era was "West End Blues," a masterpiece composed by Joseph "King" Oliver and Clarence Williams, recorded on June 28, 1928, at Okeh's Chicago studio. This legendary session featured the following personnel:

- Louis Armstrong – Trumpet and Vocals

- Earl "Fatha" Hines – piano

- Fred Robinson - trombone

- Jimmy Strong – Clarinet

- Mancy Carr – banjo

- Zutty Singleton – drums

The following is an analysis of the musical events as they unfold.

Intro 0:00 - Armstrong's trumpet cadenza showcases his virtuosity, precision, and mastery of triplet swing patterns.

A 0:13 - The first chorus of a 12-bar blues form in Eb major follows, with trumpet and clarinet engaging in a melodic dialogue. At the same time, the trombone outlines the harmonic movement, and the piano and banjo provide a staccato march-like foundation.

B 0:50 - The trombone solo begins, accompanied by the banjo's steady pulse, piano's sustained harmonic movement, and drums' triplet swing pattern on the top of the cymbal.

C 1:24 - A masterful call & response ensues between the clarinet and Armstrong's improvised scat singing, with the piano playing quarter notes and the banjo maintaining a similar style.

D 1:59 - Earl "Fatha" Hines' piano solo takes center stage with left-hand octave leaps reminiscent of ragtime. The ensemble responds with a rest, followed by Armstrong's intense solo. Hines stretches the depth of the composition with melody surges up to the 7th register of the piano.

E 2:32 - Armstrong's intense trumpet solo sustains a note over four measures and unfolds into cascading melodic lines.

E1 2:56 - The piano and trumpet engage in a cadenza dialogue, first initiated with the piano.

3:04 - Trumpet cadenza response culminating in a three-note dominant-to-tonic progression.

Coda 3:07 - The Ensemble unites with trumpet and piano.

3:14 - The drums close with a symbolic click, leaving a lasting impression.

In 1978, the induction of "West End Blues" into the Grammy Hall of Fame cemented the discography as a landmark recording, 50 years after its groundbreaking debut in 1928. Meanwhile, Louis Armstrong's innovative scat singing in his 1926 *Hot Five* recording of *Heebie Jeebies* propelled jazz into the mainstream spotlight. *The Hot Five and Hot Seven* albums between 1926 and 1928 solidified Armstrong's position as the first great jazz soloist, leaving an unforgettable footprint on the classic jazz era.

The classic jazz era was a resplendent sunburst of Black American culture, yielding explorations in Jazz transcending music. This pivotal movement gave voice to the African American experience and challenged social and political norms, fostering a sense of community and resistance. Jazz musicians found freedom and self-expression through improvisation, pushing the boundaries of creativity and vocabulary. The diverse performance traditions in African American music during this time, from New Orleans to Chicago-style jazz, urban blues to emerging gospel music, converged in a rich tapestry of sound, reflecting the complexity and beauty of Black American life.

The music from this era was a powerful catalyst for change, providing a universal language that bridged divides and inspired the practice of music. The classic jazz era's enduring legacy continues to sound with the transformative power of art and the unbridled spirit of its creators.

CHAPTER SIX

THE SWING ERA: A CULTURAL RENAISSANCE
(1930-1940)

The dawn of jazz music in the early 20th century unleashed a creative revolution, spearheaded by trumpeter Charles "Buddy" Bolden, who shattered conventions and paved the way for unbridled self-expression. A legacy of ingenuity was born as iconic trumpet masters like Bolden, Freddie Keppard, Joseph "King" Oliver, and Louis Armstrong heralded a new era of freedom through improvisation. Their bold, clarion voices pierced the veil of oppression, defiantly proclaiming the power of art to transcend the dehumanizing forces of racism.

Francis Johnson was a trailblazing African American musician who expanded the possibilities of the keyed bugle and helped shape the course of American music history. Johnson, who performed on the keyed bugle, had already pushed the boundaries of innovation during the tumultuous Antebellum period. The keyed bugle is a brass instrument that produces pitches using tone holes covered by keys on the instrument's body, unlike trumpets, which use valves to make pitches. Francis Johnson, known for his fearless experimentation with rhythm and harmony, paved the way for future generations of trumpet masters. Without his courageous contributions, the world might have been deprived of the trumpet kings who followed.

During the Classic Jazz Era (1900-1930), the trumpet reigned supreme as the leading voice in African American music and culture. Visionary trumpeters like Bolden, Keppard, Oliver, and Armstrong stood at the forefront of a community embattled by Jim Crow laws. Undaunted, they poured their hearts into their music with unwavering dedication and a joyful, unbreakable spirit. Despite the odds, their artistry continued to soar as a tower of freedom and creativity.

Paradoxically, amidst the darkness of inequality and economic devastation in 1929, during the Great Depression, jazz music ignited a rebirth that celebrated the human experience. African American artists seized control of their narrative, forging a new era of self-determination and dignity. After thirty years of an evolutionary sonic tapestry in Black American music, jazz experienced its first radical shift in musical direction. Due to the rise in individual virtuosity in jazz performance and the increase in composers writing for the jazz orchestra, the trumpet was no longer the sole representation of a leading voice in an ensemble.

The swing era witnessed the tenor saxophone's ascendance as a dominant voice in jazz, forecasting a new era of innovation. Two pioneering masters, Coleman Hawkins and Lester Young, stood at the forefront of this ascension, leaving a permanent stamp on the genre. Hawkins, revered as the "Father of the Tenor," and Young, affectionately dubbed the "President," revolutionized the instrument's expressive potential. Their contributions inspire generations, embodying a microcosm of sound, flexibility, and dexterity in intimate small groups and expansive large ensembles.

These two titans of the tenor saxophone were the first to craft a unique storytelling soundscape, weaving tales through a kaleidoscope of improvisational approaches. Yet, their styles stood in stark contrast, like opposites. Hawkins' vertical approach on the tenor saxophone unleashed a vortex of arpeggios and chordal explorations, showcasing his encyclopedic knowledge. With a mastery of complex chord progressions, Hawkins' playing was akin to that of a virtuosic architect, constructing intricate melodic structures that soared with precision and elegance. His tenor saxophone sang with a bold, declarative voice, punctuated by impeccable phrasing that left no doubt about his mastery of the idiom.

In contrast, Young's horizontal approach unfolded like a gentle breeze on a summer's day. His melodies twisted with a conversational ease that belied their underlying complexity. With a subtlety that bordered on the sublime, Young coaxed his tenor saxophone into a soft-focus haze of sweetness, warmth, and vulnerability. Young's playing was akin to that of a masterful visual artist, his brushstrokes of sound blending and merging in a luster of color and texture, forever shifting and evolving. We'll delve deeper into Lester Young's remarkable story later in this chapter.

In the mid-1920s, Coleman Hawkins embarked on a ground-breaking journey, forging a quintessential sound in jazz that would foretell an impressive body of work in the genre. As a key soloist in Fletcher Henderson's Roseland Ballroom engagements, Hawkins absorbed the genius of Louis Armstrong, Don Redman, and others, honing his craft alongside the finest musicians in New York. Like Armstrong, Hawkins possessed an expressive and soulful feel, characterized by a rich, emotional, and vibrant vibrato-laden tone. A clear tone, broad range, and daring experiments with rhythm distinguished his sound and style. Hawkins's agile and spontaneous melodic lyricist compositions continue to inspire generations of jazz artists.

Coleman Hawkins' rendition of the timeless classic "Body and Soul" is evidence of his innovative spirit. He masterfully reimagines the melody, crafting a new narrative that never once references the original written score. This tour-de-force performance showcases Hawkins' boundless creativity and influence, which extended to nearly every tenor saxophonist of his generation. Hawkins' interpretation of "Body and Soul" is jazz's most iconic saxophone solo. It's a masterclass in melodic reinvention, setting the gold standard for jazz musicians across all instruments. Moreover, Hawkins' transformative performance has had a ripple effect, elevating "Body and Soul" to the status of the most recorded song in the jazz canon, with countless artists paying homage to his ground-breaking interpretation.

Born in Woodville, Mississippi, and nurtured in New Orleans, Lester Young (1909-1959) left a significant footprint on jazz. His influence on a young Charlie Parker, eleven years his junior, was noteworthy, shaping the Alto Saxophonist's approach and laying the foundation for the future bebop revolution. While Coleman Hawkins was known for his virtuosic displays, Young's relaxed and lyrical style, characterized by a slow, warm vibrato, produced highly compelling ideas that captivated audiences. As the swing era reached its zenith in the late 1930s, Young defied convention, proving that swing didn't require volume to be commanding. His subtle, nuanced approach demonstrated that understatement could be a powerful tool in the right hands.

Two iconic compositions showcase Lester Young's improvisational genius: "Lester Leaps In" and "Jumpin' at the Woodside." The former, a jazz standard, was originally recorded by Count Basie's "Kansas City Seven" in 1939. This up-tempo AABA song form, known as rhythm changes, highlights Young's mastery of lyricism, warm sound, and intricate musical phrases. For aspiring jazz musicians, "Lester Leaps In" is a seminal study, while for enthusiasts, it's a quintessential representation of jazz at its finest. The latter, "Jumpin' at the Woodside," recorded by Count Basie Orchestra in 1938, is another signature tune showcasing Young's artistry. Interestingly, the piece was named after the historic Woodside Hotel in Harlem, a haven for jazz musicians and Negro Leagues during the segregation era of public accommodations. "Jumpin' at the Woodside" is a grand slam of jazz excellence, with Lester Young knocking it out of the park through his flawless execution of lightning-fast tempo, rhythmic precision, and crystal-clear ideas. With effortless mastery, his performances epitomize elegance, style, and grace.

Lester Young's presence was a masterclass in jazz, both sonically and stylistically. His colorful jargon and clever phrases added a layer of depth to his music, making him a true original. Young's flair for language and fashion was undeniable– he popularized the word "cool" to mean fashionable, and his double-breasted, pinstriped suits became a trademark. He coined phrases like "bread" for money, asking, "How does the bread smell?" when inquiring about gig pay. His term "the cats" showed love and respect for fellow musicians. He was incredibly creative and nicknamed the legendary Billie Holiday "Lady Day," a play on her name.

Young's influence extended beyond music to fashion, with his iconic "pork pie hat" becoming a staple for generations of artists and jazz enthusiasts. This headwear remains a beloved symbol of jazz solidarity to this day. Young's unconventional style shone through onstage– he held his saxophone at a 45-degree angle, high and to the right. When faced with racism, he'd poignantly remark, "I feel a draft." Through his music, language, and style, Lester Young left a permanent signature on the fabric of jazz. With his unparalleled originality, his impact transcends his genre, solidifying his status as a cultural icon and a legendary figure in the tenor saxophone tradition.

The jazz orchestra, an authentic American institution in its embryonic stage, conceptualized the tenor saxophone tradition, led by pioneers Lester Young and Coleman Hawkins. This tradition flourished in the early days of the emerging cultural renaissance, as the Fletcher Henderson Orchestra catapulted Hawkins' career and the Count Basie Orchestra showcased Young's genius. Duke Ellington's saxophone section, featuring Paul Gonsalves, Ben Webster, Johnny Hodges, and Harry Carney, also significantly shaped this tradition.

During the early 1900s, when jazz music took hold in American culture, the jazz orchestra did not exist. The term "orchestra" typically conjures images of European symphony orchestras, with large instrumentations of 80 to 100 musicians or more. In contrast, the jazz orchestra is a unique instrument of African American culture, characterized by improvisation and swing. A standard jazz orchestra consists of 17-20 musicians, featuring five saxophones, four trombones, four trumpets, piano, bass, and drums, with occasional guitar and vibraphone additions. Saxophonists often double on woodwind instruments like Bb clarinet, bass clarinet, flute, and soprano saxophone.

The 1930s saw the rise of the jazz orchestra as a cohesive force, popularly referred to as big bands or dance bands. Under Count Basie's and others' leadership, jazz orchestras solidified their identity, becoming synonymous with swing music. At the core of the jazz experience lies the infectious pulsation of a swing beat. Swing is the lifeblood of the ring shout celebration, fueling the music's dynamic energy and reciprocally, the dance's rhythmic propulsion. As music historian Earl Stewart notes, swing is a rhythmic concrescence, a harmonious blend of rhythms that captures the emotional character of various styles. This rhythmic synergy is essential for fully experiencing the dramatic depth of music. In essence, swing is the heart and soul of jazz music, driving physical expressions like tapping feet, clapping hands, and nodding heads in perfect sync with the rhythm.

Such a bodily response to swing made Duke Ellington remark famously, "It don't mean a thing if it *ain't got that swing.*" Similarly, James Brown's iconic "Make it funky" command highlights the intrinsic bond between music and dance, where every beat pulses with energy, accentuated by emphatic rhythms on the 'two' and 'four.'

Remarks from these iconic musicians on swing underscore the inherent connection between rhythm and dance, a fundamental principle that defines Black American music. This notion of swing, lodged in the rich traditions of the ring shout, combines shuffled rhythmic movement, the pulsation of the Pentecostal beat, and a feeling of collective momentum, purpose, and spiritual enlightenment.

Fletcher Henderson, a master composer and arranger, played a pivotal role in shaping the sound of these ensembles with his library of intricate orchestrations and dance music. Although his career faced setbacks during the Great Depression, Henderson's collaboration with the Benny Goodman Orchestra revolutionized American music. His iconic arrangements, such as "Stampede" (1926) and those written for Goodman, "King Porter Stomp," "Wrappin' It Up," "Bugle Call Rag," "Sometimes I'm Happy" and "Sing, Sing, Sing" are among a few of the Henderson arrangements that became Goodman hits. Subsequently, the 1937 Goodman recording of "Sing, Sing, Sing" was inducted into the Grammy Hall of Fame in 1982.

Swing music, an American dance phenomenon characterized by perpetual motion, symbolized racial harmony and healing during devastation, depression, and economic inequality. Following the 1929 stock market crash, swing music and dance provided a welcome escape from the financial hardships of the Great Depression, lifting the spirits of the entire nation. Despite its impact, jazz remains underappreciated for its vital contribution to American culture and its significant role in shaping character and moral fiber among its citizens.

Fletcher Henderson's impact as a bandleader, orchestrator, and architect of Goodman's commercial success as the "King of Swing" is enormous. Nevertheless, his genius often goes underrecognized. He masterfully elevated the concept of swing music by merging a soulful blueprint of an American dance craze with formal orchestral structures, creating a unique voice in jazz music. Duke Ellington understood and acknowledged Henderson's contributions with much appreciation, proclaiming him the "uncrowned king of swing."

Duke Ellington (1899-1974), the uncrowned king of music, defied categorization. Born on April 29, 1899, in Washington, D.C., he developed his craft to become one of the 20th century's greatest composers. Ellington was engaged in musical works, film scoring, theatrical productions, short poems, art paintings, and literature. His imagination and creativity transcended genres, capturing the essence of the human experience.

Ellington was a pioneer, concertizing the dreams and hopes of Black culture and broadcasting live jazz performances to a national audience. During the Harlem Renaissance (1920s-1940s), he awakened cultural identity in America. His collaborations with Billie Holiday, known for her protest blues, and Ella Fitzgerald, defined the importance of swing and improvisational music in ways that words alone could not capture. Ellington's orchestra was not just instruments; it was people with musical personalities merged into a colorful orchid of sound. From Georgia's cotton fields to Harlem's Cotton Club, Ellington and his Orchestra represented the best of Black culture.

In essence, the school of Ellington is a radical pedagogy of New Orleans musical culture, collective improvisation, call-and-response, and swing. Like Fletcher Henderson and Count Basie, Ellington's music showcased the musical aesthetics of timbre possibilities with brass and woodwind interchange and a deep range of human emotions. With over 3,000 musical compositions, Ellington's extensive work is American music's largest recorded personal jazz library. In his 50-year career, he conducted over 20,000 performances worldwide. A Carnegie Hall icon, Ellington's 1943 debut introduced his extended compositional work, *Black, Brown, and Beige,* challenging America's founding principles. He gave the following remarks to the audience:

> "We thought we wouldn't play it in its entirety tonight because it represents an awfully long and important story, and I don't think too many people are familiar with it. This is the one we dedicate to the 700 Negroes who came from Haiti to save Savannah during the Revolutionary War."

This poignant dedication underscores Ellington's commitment to celebrating overlooked chapters in African American history and his role as a cultural preservationist through music.

Ellington's music transformed attitudes about race, and he proclaimed the ascendancy of African American music. Notable works include *New World A-Comin', Liberian Suite, Perfume Suite, A Tone Parallel to Harlem,* and *Come Sunday,* featuring gospel legend Mahalia Jackson. My personal favorite works by Ellington are his 1965 Grace Cathedral premiere in San Francisco entitled *A Concert of Sacred Music,* and his 1973 sacred music premiere at London's historic Westminster Abbey.

Faithfully, Duke Ellington and his Orchestra, leading the charge in the swing era, embodied an epoch of refinement, collaborative works, and compositions beyond category.

The Swing Era was a creative explosion that transcended music, influencing fashion, dance, and art. Jazz remained steadfast as the symbol of optimism during the Great Depression, providing solace and restoration for communities pushed to the edge and rendered powerless. Swing bands emerged as a lighthouse of joy, creativity, and resistance, cementing jazz as a cornerstone of American culture and identity. The era saw the rise of iconic figures like Fletcher Henderson, Count Basie, Duke Ellington, Coleman Hawkins, Lester Young, and Benny Goodman, who revolutionized the musical terrain with the transformative power of jazz music and its ability to uplift, unite, and inspire generations.

As the curtains close on the Swing Era, we remember a cultural renaissance that swung open doors to rebirth and freedom, forever changing the rhythm of American society.

CHAPTER SEVEN

THE BOMBSHELL OF BLACK AMERICAN MUSIC

(1940-1960)

The 1940s marked a transformative era in Black American music, showcasing the rich diversity of African American cultural heritage. This pivotal decade witnessed a seismic shift in the music industry, as "race records"—previously targeted towards Black audiences—were rebranded as "Rhythm and Blues" to appeal to white listeners, perpetuating a legacy of cultural appropriation. Simultaneously, Gospel music experienced its Golden Age (1945-1955), branching into three distinct traditions within Black communities nationwide, explored later in this chapter as the solo tradition, choir tradition, and the quartet tradition. Meanwhile, jazz underwent a revolutionary metamorphosis with the emergence of bebop, a groundbreaking musical language that would redefine the genre of Jazz.

The Second World War (1939-1945) cast a shadow over the music industry, stifling the creative evolution of Black American music. While club owners found it more profitable to hire folksingers, jazz lovers became increasingly alienated. They retreated to their FM radios and phonographs, causing a downward spiral in jazz music, which led to many of the jazz orchestra's struggles to find work and placing their artistic values on hold.

The musicians' union strikes from 1942-1944 and 1948-1949, triggered by record companies' abuse of royalty payments, dealt an additional devastating blow. Iconic jazz leaders like Fletcher Henderson, Cab Calloway, Chick Webb, and others disappeared by 1948 for various reasons. Groups lost their personnel, musicians were drafted, and some volunteered for the war to stay above water, while others suffered from stress with debilitating health concerns. On face value, it would appear that Black American music lost its resilience and succumbed to societal ills.

Despite wartime challenges in the early to mid-1940s— widespread rationing, consumer shortages, and racial discrimination in war industries— the American economy experienced a remarkable surge, fueled by unprecedented war production. Millions of Americans flocked to war plants nationwide for the sole purpose of supporting war efforts. Amidst depleted morale, a vibrant musical movement emerged, significantly impacting American life. This transformation reshaped the societal fabric, creating new opportunities for Black American musicians.

Louis Jordan (1908-1975), the visionary saxophonist, vocalist, and entertainer, spearheaded the birth of Rhythm and Blues music, revolutionizing the sound of an era. At 13, Jordan performed his first gigs with the renowned Rabbit's Foot Minstrels variety troupe, a traveling entertainment show that toured the American South. Alongside his father as bandleader, Jordan experienced minstrel caricatures, comedic tales, dance, song, and staged theatrical production, exposing him to diverse audiences and shaping his early musical style. Subsequently, as his music career began to take shape, he became known as a popularizer of jump blues, an up-tempo dance-oriented hybrid of Jazz, typically performed by smaller bands. Jump music featured shouts, highly syncopated vocals, and earthy, comedic lyrics on contemporary urban themes. By the mid-1930s, Jordan's artistry had reached new heights, performing with large dance bands in New York City. His tenure with Chick Webb's Orchestra

(1936-1939) featuring Ella Fitzgerald honed his skills as an elite improviser, setting the stage for his innovative work.

Ella Fitzgerald (1947) with Dizzy, Ray Brown

Dubbed the "Father of Rhythm and Blues," Jordan merged Boogie Woogie's solo piano style with 1930s jazz orchestra dance bands, producing a distinct musical conception. R&B's characteristic lyrics mirrored the urban Black experience, reflecting lifestyles, street vernacular, and cultural nuances. Electric guitar, horns, and infectious Boogie Woogie bass patterns musically anchor Jordan's sound. Listening to Louis Jordan improvise, one can hear the legendary saxophone tradition of Coleman Hawkins and Lester Young embodied in his sound. However, his greatness as a musician connects to the authenticity of tradition, his capacity to create a visual narrative of the Black American experience, and move an audience to an emotional frenzy of joy and excitement.

Consider his provocative masterpiece, "Is You or Is You Ain't My Baby?" This iconic song title alone encapsulates the code language and metaphorical core values that defined Jordan's artistry. The guiding assumption is the feeling that you have more than one social identity, which makes it challenging to develop a sense of self. This reflective duality is a sacred macrocosm lodged deep within the African American experience, dating back to colonial America's divisive urban slave or field slave dichotomy. I dare say, "Is You or Is You Ain't My Baby?" involves a serious musical aesthetic of contemplation beyond the comedic perception of popular music.

Jordan's brilliant approach laid the foundation for R&B's dominance over the next three decades, shaping the sound of future generations. From boogie-influenced jump blues of the 1940s to the Doo Wop, Soul, and Funk revolutions through the 1970s, Rhythm and Blues chronicled the triumphs, struggles, and aspirations of African American communities.

With his landmark seven-member ensemble, the Tympani Five (founded in 1939), Jordan scored his first hits with "Knock Me a Kiss and Outskirts of Town" in 1942. His prime repertoire included protest songs like *Ration Blues*, which captured the frustrations of wartime food rationing. In 1944, "*Ration*

Blues" soared to number one on the country music and R&B charts and number 11 on the pop charts. The iconic song's opening verse and chorus begin:

[Verse 1]

Baby, baby, baby

What's wrong with Uncle Sam?

He's cut down on my sugar

Now he's messin' with my ham

[Chorus]

I got the ration blues

Blue as I can be

Oh, me, I've got those ration blues

[Verse 2]

I got to live on forty ounces

Of any kind of meat

Those forty little ounces

Gotta last me all the week

[Verse 3]

I got to cut down on my jelly

It takes sugar to make it sweet

I'm gonna steal all your jelly, baby

And rob you of your meat

[Chorus]

I got the ration blues

Blue as I can be

Oh, me, I've got those ration blues

[Verse 4]

I like to wake up in the morning

With my jelly by my side

Since rationing started, baby

You just take your stuff and hide

[Verse 5]

They reduced my meat and sugar

And rubber's disappearing fast

You can't ride no more with poppa

'Cause Uncle Sam wants my gas

[Chorus]

I got the ration blues

Blue as I can be

Oh, me, I've got those ration blues

"Caldonia Boogie," Jordan's 1945 masterpiece, epitomizes the boogie-influenced jump blues style. This classic recording boasts several notable features. The instrumentation— tenor saxophone, trumpet, upright bass, drums, and piano— pays homage to jazz's rich heritage. Distinctive musical elements catch the ear: walking bass patterns, brushes on the snare drum, hand-muted trumpet, and a robust tenor saxophone solo. Furthermore, the boogie blues progressions foreshadow the emergence of rock 'n' roll sub-genres. Additionally, the spoken word narrative and repetitive bass riffs unsuspectingly anticipate rap music's future arrival. This astonishing convergence of diverse musical elements creates a vibrant soundscape. Jordan's trademark comedic flair shines in the verse-chorus lyrics:

[Verse 1]

Walkin' with my baby, she got great big feet

She long, lean and lanky ain't had nothing to eat

But she's my baby

And I love her just the same

Crazy 'bout that woman 'cause Caldonia is her name

[Chorus]

Caldonia! Caldonia!

What make your big head so hard? Mouth

I love you, love you just the same

I'll always love you baby 'cause Caldonia is your name

[Verse 2]

You know, my mama told me to leave Caldonia alone

That's what she told me, no kidding

That's what she said, she said

"Son, keep away from that woman, she ain't no good

Don't bother with her "

But mama didn't know what Caldonia was putting down

So I'm going down to Caldonia's house

And ask her just one more time

[Chorus]

Caldonia! Caldonia!

What make your big head so hard? Mouth

I love you, love you just the same

I'll always love you baby 'cause Caldonia is your name

In 1993, Louis Jordan's "Caldonia Boogie" or "Caldonia" was inducted into the Grammy Hall of Fame. In 2013, the U.S. National Recording Registry added the song to a list of significant songs that culturally, historically, and aesthetically reflect life in the United States.

Other notable songs include "Saturday Night Fish Fry," "Choo Choo Ch'Boogie," "Ain't Nobody Here But Us Chickens," and "Let the Good Times Roll." This prolific catalog of material solidified his legacy as a master storyteller, utilizing comedic narratives to captivate audiences. Jordan's influence extended far beyond R&B. As a consummate entertainer, he reigned as the king of jukebox technology and pioneered film shorts, known as "soundies," precursors to modern music videos.

Rhythm and Blues gained greater popularity, raising questions about the complex dynamics of cultural exchange and appropriation. As Black artists' music gains mainstream attention, it often gets rebranded and marketed to broader audiences, sometimes without proper recognition or compensation for its creators. Historically, this phenomenon highlights the tension between cultural appreciation and cultural exploitation.

Cultural Appropriation of Black American Music: A Legacy of Exploitation

Cultural appropriation, a pervasive form of oppression, involves members of dominant cultures exploiting and profiting from minority cultures without acknowledgment and compensation. This phenomenon has plagued Black culture since the 19th-century minstrelsy, when racist white performers generated wealth by donning blackface to mock and demean African Americans during productions both in theatre and film. Notorious examples include:

- **Thomas "Daddy" Rice** (1808-1860) popularized blackface performances, appropriating African American vernacular speech, song, and dance.

- **Stephen Foster** (1826-1864), dubbed "The Father of American Music," built his fame on parlor and blackface minstrelsy performances during the pre-Civil War era.

- **Al Jolson** (1886-1950), the "King of Blackface," extracted African American music and tailored it for white American audiences, becoming one of the highest-paid entertainers of the 1920s.

This exploitative practice persisted for over a century, with even the BBC (British Broadcasting Corporation) airing "The Black and White Minstrel Show" until 1978, on the cusp of hip-hop's emergence. Minstrelsy normalized cultural appropriation and the image of Black performers entertaining white audiences while excluding them from these events. Historically, cultural appropriation of Black artists' innovative music, dating back to the beginning of ragtime music shortly after the Civil War, has perpetuated a harmful cycle. In the American music industry, when white artists cover and popularize Black artists' songs, the original Black versions of those songs are erased from the fabric of American music. The evolution of cultural appropriation, including minstrelsy, remains ingrained in American culture and is problematic, as it has long since plagued rhythm and blues artists, depriving Black artists of recognition and compensation for decades. Today, this phenomenon extends beyond music to fashion, dance, language, and various forms of cultural expression, perpetuating systemic inequality. A few instances of cultural appropriation are further highlighted:

Big Mama Thornton: The Original "Hound Dog" Artist

Willie Mae "Big Mama" Thornton (1926-1984) was a trailblazing harmonica player, singer, and songwriter. Her authentic rhythm and blues style embodied the rich cultural heritage of Black American music during the Civil Rights Movement. Thornton's 1952 hit *Hound Dog* sold 500,000 copies, laying the basis for rock 'n' roll.

However, Elvis Presley's 1956 "Hound Dog" cover sold 10 million copies, catapulting him to fame without proper credit to Thornton. Despite her originality, Thornton received only one royalty check for $500. The song's estimated lifetime earnings are $4.3 billion and counting.

Little Richard: The Architect of Rock 'n' Roll

Richard Wayne "Little Richard" Penniman (1932-2020) wrote and recorded "Tutti Frutti" in 1955. This revolutionary song merged gospel, boogie-woogie, and blues with an assertive rock beat. Producer Robert "Bumps" Blackwell recognized its impact on rock music.

Yet, Pat Boone's cover of "Tutti Frutti" in 1956 achieved greater success on the pop charts, exemplifying the unfair practice of remaking Black recordings for White audiences. Boone also recorded Little Richard's "Long Tall Sally," "Ready Teddy," "Lucille," and "Keep A Knockin." In the documentary, *Hail, Hail, Rock 'n' Roll,* Little Richard expressed his frustration: "When Pat Boone recorded my music, I was angry."

Big Joe Turner: The King of Rock 'n' Roll

Joseph Vernon "Big Joe" Turner, Jr. (1911-1985) was a trailblazing musician whose 1954 recording of "Shake, Rattle, and Roll" topped the U.S. Billboard Rhythm and Blues (R&B) chart. However, record labels employed an exploitative practice called "mainlining" to profit from R&B music among white audiences that involved hiring white artists to sanitize and re-record songs originally performed by Black artists.

Case in point: Bill Haley and His Comets released a cover of "Shake, Rattle, and Roll" the same week Turner's version reached #1 on the Billboard charts, marking the beginning of a disturbing trend. Black American music was repackaged for white audiences, disregarding its originality, social context, and cultural significance. Turner's experience was not isolated. This exploitative practice continued, depriving Black artists of rightful recognition and compensation.

Fats Domino: Rock 'n' Roll Pioneer

Antoine Caliste "Fats" Domino, Jr. (1928-2017), the legendary New Orleans musician, paved the way for rock 'n' roll. With 65 million records sold, Domino's impact on the genre is undeniable. Two of his iconic hits, "Ain't That a Shame" and "Blueberry Hill," released by Imperial Records in 1955, soared to success, selling over 1 million copies. However, Pat Boone quickly capitalized on Domino's momentum, recording "Ain't That a Shame" later that year. Boone's version became his first #1 single on Billboard, exemplifying the exploitative practice of cultural appropriation that often overshadowed Black artists' achievements.

Chuck Berry: The Father of Rock 'n' Roll

Charles Edward Anderson Berry (1926-2017), the visionary musician, established his legacy as the Father of "Rock 'n' Roll." His innovative sound and style inspired icons like The Rolling Stones and the Beatles. Berry's signature "Duckwalk" dance and hits like "Maybellene" (1955) and "Johnny B. Goode" (1958) transcended racial boundaries, achieving mainstream success and temporarily disrupting the music industry's exploitative "mainlining" practice.

Unfortunately, mainlining focused on marketing and promoting a "pop taste"–often leading to a substantial decline in traditional musical skills and values.

From Chuck Berry's humble beginnings at 2520 Goode Avenue in St. Louis, Missouri, Berry rose to global superstardom, influencing legends like Bruce Springsteen, Aerosmith, Jimi Hendrix, AC/DC, Buddy Holly, The Beach Boys, Ernie Isley, Prince, and countless others. However, music critic Todd "Stereo" Williams notes that by the 1970s, rock 'n' roll had propelled white artists to fame and fortune, often at the expense of Black artists who originated the genre. This cultural appropriation perpetuated exploitation, erasure, and inequality.

African American music genres, including R&B and others, are commonly connected to Black music traditions and have faced issues of cultural appropriation. Despite its sacred and spiritual nature, many white artists borrowed Black gospel music to build wealth. While cultural exchange can be enriching, appropriation without proper understanding, respect, or credit can be problematic for disenfranchised communities.

Black American Gospel Music: A Legacy of Faith and Song

In the 1920s, Black American Gospel Music drew from African American folk traditions like spirituals, ring shouts, and work songs, evolving into a blues-infused religious style. By the 1940s, Black Gospel music had defined the sound of 20th-century Black American music, characterized by vibrant hand clapping, soulful lead vocals, and spirited choir responses.

The foundations of Gospel Music began with Charles Albert Tindley (1851-1933), who laid the groundwork for Black Gospel music with his prolific composition of gospel hymns in the early 1900s. His iconic hymns include but are not limited to: "Stand by Me," "The Storm is Passing Over," " Leave it There," and "We'll Understand it By and By." These hymns became staples of the Black Gospel music genre and influenced generations of Gospel musicians, including Thomas A. Dorsey, the Father of Gospel Music.

Thomas A. Dorsey (1899-1993) transformed Gospel music, drawing inspiration from Charles Albert Tindley. But before becoming the pioneer of Gospel, Dorsey honed his craft as bluesman "Georgia Tom," touring with the legendary Ma Rainey from 1924 to 1928. Dorsey's breakthrough came in 1928 with his blues hit record "It's Tight Like That." Working alongside Ma Rainey, the "Mother of the Blues," refined his skills in piano comping, composing, crafting arrangements, and developing a signature style. Dorsey's musical footprint ignited his vision of blending sacred texts with secular blues. This emerging radical sound shattered traditional church music boundaries, heralding the "Golden Age of Gospel Music." His contributions are immeasurable as he:

- Coined the term "Gospel Song"
- Organized the first gospel choir at Pilgrim Baptist Church in Chicago (1931), where he served for 50 years
- Co-founded the first gospel choir at Ebenezer Missionary Baptist Church in Chicago (1931)
- Co-founded the National Convention of Gospel Choirs and Choruses, NCGCC (1933)
- Shaped the solo gospel blues idiom
- Composed timeless classics: "Take My Hand, Precious Lord" and "Peace in the Valley"

The Golden Age of Black Gospel Music (1945-1955)

After World War II, Gospel music exploded onto the national scene, spreading like wildfire through radio, recordings, and concerts by traveling gospel singers. From iconic venues like New York's Apollo Theater and Los Angeles' Shrine Auditorium to cities across America— Philadelphia, Detroit, St. Louis, Cleveland, Louisville, Chicago, Oakland, and more— Gospel music reached people's hearts everywhere. Three distinct performance traditions emerge in Gospel music, showcasing the genre's remarkable diversity: solo tradition, gospel quartet tradition, and choir/choral styles.

The Solo Tradition

Rooted in a blues-influenced idiom with embellished and elongated notes accentuated with rhythmic clapping and shouts, the Solo tradition traces back to Thomas A. Dorsey's influential gospel blues sound. His creative output in the Gospel's Golden Age produced many compositional masterpieces. Standard repertoire includes "If You See My Savior," "Peace in the Valley," "Lord Has Laid His Hand on Me," "Jesus Rose Again," "I'm a Pilgrim," and many others. This intensely musical expression showcased a powerhouse of gospel singers' deep connection with God. Dorsey's 1932 classic, "Take My Hand, Precious Lord," epitomized this tradition. Legendary Solo gospel artists include the following. However, this is not an exhaustive list:

- Sally Martin, "Mother of Gospel Music" and NCGCC co-founder
- Theodore Frye organized the first gospel choir with Dorsey at Ebenezer Missionary Baptist Church in Chicago (1931) and had a reputation as a singer who could move the house
- Mahalia Jackson, undisputed "Queen of Gospel Music"

- Magnolia Lewis Butts, unsung hymnist and composer in Black Gospel music

- Arizona Dranes, known as the first gospel pianist

- Roberta Martin, Dorsey's pianist at Pilgrim Baptist church in Chicago, Illinois (1932)

- Sister Rosetta Tharpe, the first gospel guitarist and solo artist to popularize gospel blues

Other notable Black Gospel Music singers and songwriters in the solo performance tradition are as follows:

- Albertina Walker

- James Cleveland

- Dorothy Norwood

- Aretha Franklin

Thomas Dorsey's leadership and mentorship in the solo tradition of Gospel music helped create a powerful and spirit-filled sound representative of Black preaching, stretching beyond the pews into the souls of many.

The Gospel Quartet Tradition

In Gospel music, the quartet tradition shines with "a cappella" singing, exhibiting impeccable four-part harmony. Typically, male vocal ensembles perform without accompaniment, occasionally using their voices to create rhythmic grooves, growls, slurs, humming, and falsetto pitches. Their repertoire includes Jubilee spirituals, Gospel hymns, and original compositions by Lucie E. Campbell, W. Herbert Brewster, and Thomas A. Dorsey.

Rooted in African American folk traditions and Negro spirituals, Gospel quartets share similarities to the Jubilee Quartet tradition inaugurated by the renowned Fisk University Jubilee Quartet (1909). Early Black groups emerged from Black higher education institutions later known as Historically Black Colleges and Universities (HBCUs), including Hampton Normal and Agricultural Institute, Tuskegee Normal and Industrial Institute, Utica Institute, Howard University, and Morehouse College. All of which drew inspiration from Fisk University's Jubilee Quartet legacy. Gospel Quartets in the 1940s represent characteristics such as:

- "A cappella" singing

- Four-part harmony

- Male voices

- Personalized expressions

- Improvisation/Ad lib

- Recitation

- Jazz-influenced scat singing

The best resource of the "Gospel Quartet Tradition," contrasting the "Jubilee Quartet Tradition," is characterized in the following examples of landmark recordings:

- Fisk Jubilee Singers: "Swing Low, Sweet Chariot" (1909)

- Fisk Jubilee Singers: "Ezekiel Saw De Wheel" (1926)

- The Golden Gate Quartet: "Swing Down Chariot" (1940)

- The Golden Gate Quartet: "God told Nicodemus" (1941)

In 1934, Norfolk, Virginia's Booker T. Washington High School produced a musical phenomenon– The Golden Gate Jubilee Singers, later renamed The Golden Gate Quartet. Four teenage friends– Willie Johnson (baritone), William Langford (tenor), Henry Owens (second tenor), and Orlandus Wilson (bass), fueled by passion and talent, developed a collective footprint on the pages of Gospel music history. Their innovative style blended non-verbal expressions, dynamic bodily movements, special vocal effects imitating train sounds, ostinato bass patterns, humming, and theatrical narrations. As the most celebrated Gospel quartet of the Golden Age, they paved the way for Rhythm and Blues' (R&B) "Doo Wop" style, alongside:

- The Mills Brothers

- The Ink Spots

- Little Anthony & The Imperials

Other legendary Gospel quartets include:

- The Silver Leaf Quartet

- The Harmonizing Four

- The Dixie Hummingbirds

- The Blind Boys of Alabama

- The Soul Stirrers (featuring Sam Cooke, "Father of Soul Music")

Choir/Choral Styles: Dynamic Call-and-Response

The choir/choral tradition is a style that embodies a vibrant, blues-infused religious idiom, mirroring the solo tradition's emotional intensity. This soulful style, characterized by personalized expressions of praise, was accompanied by percussion instruments, piano, Hammond organ, and mixed voices. Song arrangements, frequently structured in a chorus/verse format, are designed to build excitement and transformative power from the choir and the designated featured solo vocalist. However, in the Black church, spontaneous creativity reigns supreme. I've witnessed directors unexpectedly choose a choir member not previously selected or invite a gifted person sitting in the congregation to lead a song, unleashing an unforgettable moment. This dynamic choir tradition represents the essence of Black worship: anticipation meets divine surprise. Every gathering promises a unique blessing, as the Spirit orchestrates a high praise.

Additionally, a director may employ the "swing lead" technique, where two singers are selected to lead one song, creating a triangulated melodic phrase between soloists and choir responses. This conception is similar to jazz instrumentalists trading improvisational choruses within the song structure. Ultimately, the dynamic call-and-response interaction between lead solo voices and spirited choirs forms the cornerstone of exceptional Gospel music in this traditional performance style.

The Philadelphia Gospel Sound: A National Movement

Philadelphia trailblazed the East Coast gospel movement, embracing Thomas Dorsey's visionary style and gospelizing African American church music nationwide. Building on Chicago's momentum, the city catapulted female groups to prominence in the 1940s. The Davis Sisters dramatically reshaped gospel music with their bold, hard gospel sound, characterized by note bends, spirited shouts, and soulful growls. Meanwhile, the Clara Ward Singers mesmerized audiences with vamp device techniques, masterfully repeating choruses with incredibly riveting effects.

However, the Christian Tabernacle Church of God in Christ choir epitomized the Philadelphia sound during gospel's Golden Age. Their exuberant performances showcased the infectious gospel beat, punctuated by hand-clapping pulsations, robust tambourine playing, and organ accompaniment, laying the foundation for soul-stirring vocals. Their dynamic singing style symbolized the essence of Philadelphia gospel, spreading an irresistible spirit of praise. Moreover, the gospel sound in Philly became very popular due to local record companies and influential disc jockeys promoting the hometown sound throughout the nation.

The Gospel Sound of Detroit

Rev. C.L. Franklin (1915-1984), a charismatic preacher, civil rights activist, and gifted singer, pastored New Bethel Baptist Church from 1946 to 1976. Under his leadership, the church became a hub for gospel music in Detroit, attracting legendary artists like Mahalia Jackson, Clara Ward, Sam Cooke, Cissy Houston, Nat King Cole, Jackie Wilson, and Sarah Vaughan. The Caravans also frequented the church, featuring Albertina Walker, Inez Williams, Shirley Caesar, and James Cleveland. Additionally, Cleveland, hailed as the "King of Gospel," served as organist and music director in the early 1960s, leading the way with fusing traditional Black gospel with jazz harmonies in mass choir arrangements.

Gospel music in Detroit personified Black excellence and civil rights activism. Alongside the Black-owned Motown recording company (1959) and the artistry of Smokey Robinson, Stevie Wonder, The Miracles, The Jackson Five, The Temptations, the Four Tops, The Supremes, and Marvin Gaye, a new transformation evolved in Black American music fueled by the Church and the good news of the gospel. Rev. Franklin's daughter, Aretha Franklin (1942-

2018), began singing in the church choir at age 9, showcasing her prodigious talent as a soloist. Her 1956 live recording of Thomas Dorsey's "Take My Hand, Precious Lord" at New Bethel Baptist Church demonstrated her remarkable skills, impeccable timing, lyric improvisational prowess, elongated phrasing, and pitch control far beyond her precocious 14 years of age.

Aretha Franklin's piano performance exemplified a master class on gospel music accompaniment. Her embellishments fashioned a masterful piano narrative clothed in the oral storytelling tradition. Moreover, the live interaction between Aretha and the congregation–"Yes Lord!" shouts and passionate praise responses revealed a compelling sense of support and connection with God.

Unsurprisingly, Aretha's evolution into the "Queen of Soul" in the 1960s was encouraged by a lineage of great singers and songwriters, including her mentors Ray Charles, the Father of Soul music, and Sam Cooke. Aretha's gospel roots remained evident, as captured on the iconic album entitled "Aretha Gospel" (Chess-CH-91521).

Mattie Moss Clark (1925-1994): Pioneer of the Gospel Choir Sound

Dr. Mattie Moss Clark left a significant footprint on the advancement of gospel music. As Minister of Music for the Church of God in Christ (COGIC) denomination's Southwest Michigan Jurisdiction and International Music Department, she served with distinction for over 25 years. During her tenure, Dr. Clark founded the International Mass Choir and performed annually at the United National Auxiliary Convention (UNAC). Dr. Clark founded Midnight Musicals as a gifted builder of Gospel music institutions and a highly respected instructor, nurturing numerous future gospel stars under her expert tutelage. A short list of luminaries, such as The Hawkins Family, Andrae and Sandra Crouch, Rance Allen, and the Clark Sisters, achieved superstardom and legendary status.

However, a landmark moment in Gospel music history came in 1958 when Dr. Clark recorded her inaugural "Going to Heaven to Meet the King" with the Southwest Michigan State Choir. This pioneering work introduced what gospel music scholars call a multi-part harmony style for mass choirs, now a touchstone in Gospel music. The Mattie Moss Clark training method comes from an intense oral traditional practice of storytelling. Known to be a tough taskmaster and sometimes temperamental, she focused her rehearsals on teaching members their sectional harmony parts in isolation before uniting them. Consequently, choir members are expected to memorize the words and musical notes without the aid of written sheet music. Performances are presented with vocal dynamics and heartfelt expressions of love.

Reflections

During my musical journey through gospel ecosystems, I discovered a captivating parallel between Johann Sebastian Bach's intricate 17th-century contrapuntal fugues and the multi-part harmony style in 20th-century Black gospel music. This epiphany began in the late 1980s on a Sunday morning at Allen Temple Baptist Church in Oakland, California, where I served as orchestra music director. The church's pastors, J. Alfred Smith Sr. and J. Alfred Smith Jr., were exceptional preachers and free-spirited musicians who encouraged improvisation and creative freedom among musicians. The church organist, Anthony Williams, mesmerized the congregation with spontaneous improvisation and high praise. Moved by the Spirit, he would leap from the organ and run down the church's main aisle and out the door. I affectionately called him Bishop, as he skillfully wove together thematic hymns, classical nuances, jazz undertones, and soulful expressions with gospel fervor, all tied together seamlessly by melodic imitations, creating a miraculous moment in the worship experience.

Famed world-class composer, pianist, and arranger Richard Smallwood skillfully illustrates this innovative concept, blending intricate counterpoint and soulful harmonies. His iconic pieces, such as "Anthem of Praise," "Bless the Lord," "Total Praise," and "The Center of My Joy," exemplify the seamless fusion of classical and gospel music traditions that are trademarks of his artistry. This captivating journey reverberated in the mid-to-late 1990s, albeit somewhat differently, with the renowned Walter Hawkins, Love Center Choir, and Love Center Church in Oakland, California. Their contrasting harmonies resonated deeply, reaffirming the connection between Bach's counterpoint conception and Black Gospel's soulful, layered timbres.

As aforementioned, Dr. Clark's influential multi-part harmonic practice involved a unique structural approach, showcasing each vocal section independently in isolation before uniting them. This seemingly simple probing process unfolded in four stages. First, the soprano section (high female voices) sang their specific part. Second, the alto section (lower female voices) sang their part in isolation. Third, the tenor section (male voices) sang from the soprano and alto parts in isolation. Finally, all three sections merged, creating a rich, layered melodic and harmonic style. In this dynamic format, rhythm section instruments such as tambourines, drums, cymbals, and keyboards typically enter after the sections unite, although optional percussive elements might accompany each sectional part. In many instances, congregational handclapping increased the energy and sound. Dr. Clark's innovation transcended traditional structures, defining distinct roles for soprano, alto, and tenor voices in mass choir settings. To fully experience this colorful gospel form, attend a live Black church worship service on any Sunday.

Dr. Clark's gospel choir expertise propelled her to train numerous ensembles across the Church of God in Christ (COGIC) community, making her a highly sought-after mentor. In early 1968, she joined forces with James Cleveland, inviting him as a special guest to lead a groundbreaking 1,000-voice mass choir in a Sing-O-Rama symposium. Held at Reverend C. L. Franklin's New Bethel Baptist Church in Detroit, this pivotal event aimed to perpetuate gospel music's legacy through powerful performance and education. Dr. Clark's mentorship inspired many, including James Cleveland, who founded the renowned Gospel Music Workshop of America (GMWA) convention in August 1968 at King Solomon Baptist Church in Detroit.

It is imperative to recognize and acknowledge innovative Gospel Black American music publishers, especially those of the 1940s and 1950s, including Thomas A. Dorsey Publishing, Theodore Frye Publishing, Sally Martin and Kenneth Morris Music Publishing Company (1940), Lillian Bowles Music House, Emma L. Jackson Studio, and Charles H. Price Publishers. These trailblazers ignited a movement to preserve Black Gospel Music's heritage in America, empowering gospel artists creatively and economically. The National Convention of Gospel Choirs and Choruses (1933), National Baptist Convention (1948), Gospel Music Workshops of America (1969), and COGIC Midnight Musicals led the charge in galvanizing publishers to network and continue expanding the gospel reach beyond boundaries. Thomas Dorsey and Willie Mae Ford Smith of St. Louis provided leadership and national support, inspiring communities like Cleveland and Louisville.

Derby City: A Hub for Gospel Music

The city of Louisville in Kentucky has a storied history. Known as the Derby City, Louisville is the home of Muhammad Ali, the greatest boxer of all time and global humanitarian, and Simmons College of Kentucky, the first Black institution of higher education founded to educate newly emancipated Black people, and recognized as a Historically Black College and University (HBCU). Simmons College of Kentucky– Louisville's only HBCU, and America's first comeback institution, opened in 1879, when Black jockeys dominated the Kentucky Derby, winning six times between 1890 and 1899. However, another powerful characteristic of the city is its rich legacy of faith-based communities.

Louisville's Black gospel faith traditions are rooted in institutions, community engagement, national and local conventions, and talented artists preserving the gospel story. Legendary Gospel music historian, producer, and songwriter Wilma Clayborn, alongside her husband John, owned and operated Grace Gospel Records. Their grandson, Jason Clayborn, continues the legacy as an acclaimed songwriter, vocal arranger, and worship leader. A Dove and Stella Award nominee, Jason Clayborn's exceptional vocals are in high demand. As worship leader at St. Stephen Baptist Church in Louisville, he showcases the city's gospel heritage and his love for music ministry. The box set, *I'm Glad About It: The Legacy of Gospel Music in Louisville,* documents Louisville's invaluable contributions to gospel music history.

St. Stephen Baptist Church Music Ministry

In Louisville, Kentucky, St. Stephen Baptist Church's music ministry embodies the finest aspects of Black Gospel Music. This celebrated department expertly executes contemporary gospel hymns, anthems, and spirituals precisely. Directors, band leaders, and musicians collaborate to shape the performance tradition of various choir styles and musical accompaniment.

The complexities of Gospel Music evoke robust responses, considering factors like selection of musical pieces, word content, rhythm, tempo, and melody. Effective directors prioritize musicians' personalized gifts. Minister Kevin James– St. Stephen Baptist Church's exceptional Minister of Music at all three church campuses, including Louisville, Kentucky, Jeffersonville, Indiana, and Radcliff, Kentucky– exemplifies visionary leadership with over 38 years in the ministry, helping "lay down the track" for musicians to spread the gospel. Minister James balances preservation and innovation, recognizing the importance of traditional hymns like Charles Wesley's 16th-century classic, "A Charge to Keep I Have," when he emphasizes the following verse:

- *To serve the present age*

- *My calling to fulfill*

- *May in all my power engage*

- *To do my Master's will*

This ministerial approach ensures the next generation appreciates the heritage of Black Gospel Music. Another influential work is Isaac Watts' 1707 publication, *Hymns and Spiritual Songs.* Watts eloquently penned these words, expressing the need for the Holy Spirit's invigorating power to fulfill our journey through life and effective music ministry:

- *Come Holy Spirit, Heavenly dove,*

- *With all thy quickening powers,*

- *Kindle a flame of sacred love,*

- *In these cold hearts of ours.*

Without the Holy Spirit, Gospel Music loses its power. Brian Lofton, esteemed Music Director formerly with Chicago's Sweet Holy Spirit Combined Choirs, now at St. Stephen Baptist Church, understands the importance of kindling a flame of sacred love "in these cold hearts of ours." He emphasizes three key fundamental characters that his musicians must acknowledge: Be attentive, less is more, and play from the heart. Brian Lofton describes a philosophical yet straightforward framework for an effective organic music ministry of healing, reconciliation, and transformation.

In summary, history reveals the early convergence of Rhythm and Blues (R&B) and Gospel music that sparked a cultural explosion, propelling African American music onto the national stage. As diverse performance traditions flourished, so did fostering innovation and artistic expression from musicians. As a result, Gospel and R&B became cornerstones of American music, transcending genres and shaping the course of music history.

As shared, the 1940s bombshell transformation of Black American music in America ignited a lasting legacy, reshaping African American musical identity. This pivotal era's contributions—from pioneers like Mahalia Jackson and Thomas A. Dorsey to the emergence of Gospel choirs and R&B groups—continue to inspire generations. Black artists' impact extends beyond music, influencing social justice movements and cementing African American cultural relevance.

In conclusion, early R&B and Gospel revolution yielded significant contributions: the rise of Gospel choirs, R&B's popular appeal, and iconic storytellers like Sam Cooke and Mahalia Jackson. This era's social-political implications—advocating for racial equality and freedom—remain poignant. As confirmation of music's resolute power, the Golden Age of Gospel remains vital in African American cultural heritage.

Chapter EIGHT

BEBOP: A Jazz Quintet Legacy

(1945-1960)

The Jazz Quintet tradition is deeply rooted in the Black American community, with a rich cultural heritage shaped by innovative stylistic developments and rising stars in Jazz music. As musicians sought to expand their musical refinement, mobility, and personal growth, a new identity and musical language emerged in the 1940s, coinciding with the Harlem Renaissance's outpouring of literature, art, and music.

This artistic ferment in Black America, which began in the 1920s and 1930s, created a residue of inspiration and self-determination that culminated in the 1940s jazz explosion. Bebop, a musical movement that embodied urbanity, challenged artists to make subtle changes in nuance, clarity, finesse, and fine-tuning of a musical lineage originating in Black Folk genres.

As bebop musicians celebrated and honored jazz music's growth, sophistication, artistry, and maturation, they remained committed to preserving its authenticity. The jazz quintet legacy, exemplified by bebop, represents this paradigm.

To understand the jazz quintet sound, exploring its evolutionary context is essential. The modern jazz quintet, which emerged in the 1940s, typically consists of a traditional trio– piano, upright bass, and drums– augmented by any combination of two instruments, such as guitar, trumpet, saxophone, flute, or trombone. Post-1945, the standard instrumentation features trumpet, saxophone, piano, upright bass, and drums, becoming the signature aggregation that has endured well into the 21st century.

In contrast, early New Orleans jazz, pre-1930s, employed six or more players, incorporating combinations of clarinets, trombones, and trumpets, alongside rhythm section instruments. Charles "Buddy" Bolden, jazz's creator, formed his New Orleans group with six players, establishing the first jazz band around 1895. However, Louis Armstrong's Hot Five recording group marked a pivotal shift from Bolden's conception of jazz instrumentation during the mid-1920s.

Armstrong's ensemble of five players, consisting of trumpet, clarinet, trombone, piano, and banjo, inadvertently spawned the modern jazz quintet era of the 1940s. Armstrong's conception of the Hot Five identity, even if serendipitously, sparked the emergence of the post-1940s jazz quintet movement. The trumpet-saxophone-piano-bass-drums combination forged a new jazz identity and a distinct cultural renaissance in jazz music.

This quintet sound, emerging in the 1940s, ushered in a revolutionary era known as bebop, transforming jazz music forever. Bebop's emphasis on speed, complexity, and improvisation raised the bar for jazz musicians, and its influence remains felt today.

The Mainstream of Jazz: Bebop

Bebop, a revolutionary jazz style, emerged as the mainstream of jazz music in the 1940s. Characterized by its distinctive quintet sound, featuring alto saxophone, trumpet, piano, upright bass, and drums, bebop pioneered a new era led by Charlie Parker (1920-1955), Dizzy Gillespie (1917-1993), and Thelonious Monk (1917-1982). Bebop emerged from musicians' desire for limitless improvisational freedom, which was unavailable in the 1930s dance bands. This aspiration led to jam sessions, fostering unrestrained creativity. Consequently, bebop became jazz's first non-dancing style, requiring intense listener engagement. The drums' rhythmic and melodic approach drives the ensemble's innovative language. Building on bebop's foundation, limitless improvisation and unrestrained creativity evolved through hard bop, neo-bop, and beyond, solidifying the jazz quintet's enduring legacy.

Dizzy Gillespie 1946 "Famous Door" NYC

The jazz quintet legacy evolves as a continuum, elevating the musical arts' cultural significance while reflecting society's social-political impact on the human spirit. Visionary artists united to safeguard their art's authenticity and cultural values across generations. Many believed society's potential hinges on humanity's collective worth. During World War II's turmoil, beboppers conveyed radical tension through faster tempos, improvisational extensions, and harmonic complexities. The school bebop promoted:

- Public and private jam sessions

- Harlem rent parties

- One-on-one mentoring among jazz musicians

Jam sessions provided an experimental laboratory for improvisation and musical growth.

During this era, Minton's Playhouse in Harlem, located at 201 W 118th Street, became the epicenter of this innovative institution. Minton's Playhouse was a popular place that nurtured bebop culture and was credited as the birthplace of modern music. The club's original owner, Henry Minton, the first Black delegate to the American Federation of Musicians Local 802, has a storied history of generosity with food and loans, making his establishment a favorable hangout for musicians. Because of his union relations, Henry Minton ensured musicians were not fined for their participation in jam sessions, which the union prohibited.

Minton's Playhouse offered immunity for patrons and a sanctuary for jazz musicians, fostering a community of respect and humility. Author and literary critic Ralph Ellison described Minton's Playhouse as a homogeneous community where a collectivity of everyday experiences could find continuity and meaningful expression.

Early Bebop Pioneers: Revolutionizing Jazz

The 1940s jam sessions bred visionary musicians who prioritized artistic integrity over entertainment. The musicians acquired a thirst for creating something more challenging and exhilarating than any music of their generation. These bebop pioneers– Charlie Parker, Dizzy Gillespie, Thelonious Monk, Bud Powell, Kenny Clarke, Max Roach, Oscar Pettiford, and Miles Davis– sought excellence, rejecting commercial exploitation and stereotypical imagery reminiscent of 19th-century minstrelsy. Early modern jazz pioneers wanted to reverse the parasitic relationship that non-Black commercial forces had historically had on Black American music. The early bebop pioneers did not look favorably upon musicians who commercially exploited the music with no concern for its artistic merit.

Charlie Parker, Miles Davis, Tommy Potter, Duke Jordan, Max Roach, @ the Three Deuces 1947

Musical Innovation

Harlem's vibrant artistic culture ignited an improvisation phenomenon: explosive lyricism, complex chord changes, and rapid tonal shifts, underscored by a driving ride cymbal beat. Bebop's progenitors craved innovation, pushing boundaries and revolutionizing jazz music. Dizzy Gillespie explained his unique improvisational approach of combining legato and staccato notes as one phrase. Dizzy explained that when listening to musicians improvise, some notes are rhythmically attacked, and some are slurred. According to Dizzy's perspective on improvisation, Bebop music necessitated rigorous study to articulate complex techniques, demanding attentive and critically engaged listening skills.

"KoKo": A Masterpiece

Charlie Parker's 1945 magnum opus, "KoKo," exemplifies bebop's artistry. This iconic piece showcases Parker's melodic genius, with lightning-fast phrases and improvisational mastery. "KoKo" remains one of jazz's most studied saxophone solos, preserving Parker's unique legacy as a highly influential soloist and leading figure in the development of bebop.

The Quintet ensemble features:

- Charlie Parker: Alto Saxophone

- Dizzy Gillespie: Trumpet & Piano

- Bud Powell: Piano

- Max Roach: Drums

- Curley Russell: Bass

On November 26, 1945, Charlie Parker led a landmark recording session for Savoy Records at WOR Studios in New York City, billed as the "Greatest Jazz Session Ever." This session followed the lifting of the AFM's recording ban.

Session Details:

- Date: November 26, 1945
- Location: WOR Studios, New York City
- Label: Savoy Records

Artists:

- Charlie Parker: Alto Saxophone
- Miles Davis: Trumpet
- Curley Russell: Bass
- Dizzy Gillespie: Piano
- Max Roach: Drums

Selected Tracks Recorded by Charlie Parker:

- "Now is the Time"
- "Billie's Bounce"

Miles Davis' Debut

Miles Davis made his recording debut with Charlie Parker as a young trumpeter. Davis first met Parker and Dizzy in July of 1944 while performing with Billy Eckstine's Orchestra at Club Riviera in St. Louis, Missouri. Miles Davis will be explored later in this chapter.

Billy Eckstine and Nelson Riddle, NYC 1948

Also known as the most outstanding concert ever, featuring a group simply known as The Quintet:

- Charlie Parker: Alto saxophone
- Dizzy Gillespie: Trumpet
- Bud Powell: Piano
- Charles Mingus: Bass
- Max Roach: Drums

May 1953 marked the historic Massey Hall concert, dubbed "The Greatest Concert Ever." Despite logistical challenges, five jazz giants – The Quintet – united for a once-in-a-lifetime performance. Unlike traditional recordings, which often feature false starts, alternate takes, and polished precision, the Massey Hall concert shines as a spontaneous, raw-energy masterpiece. This iconic performance showcased Charlie Parker alongside bebop's brightest stars, delivering a cohesive, uninterrupted display of improvisational genius.

Massey Hall Concert Setlist

The highly esteemed Charlie Parker-Dizzy Gillespie Quintet performed the following pieces live at Massey Hall:

1. "Perdido" - Composer: Juan Tizol (1941) Opening number, eliciting enthusiastic applause from jazz aficionados

2. "Salt Peanuts" - Composer: Dizzy Gillespie (1942) Charlie Parker's eloquent introduction of this composition offered witty amusement: "At this time we would like to play a tune composed by my worthy

constituent Mr. Dizzy Gillespie in the year of 1942. We sincerely hope you do enjoy 'Salt Peanuts.'"

3. "All the Things You Are" - Composer: Jerome Kern (1939) Parker's saxophone introduction, Gillespie's soulful "A" section melody, Parker returns in the bridge section, Mingus' walking bass lines, and Max Roach's superb stylistic brushwork

4. "Wee" (A.K.A. Allen's Alley) - Composer: Denzil Best Showcases quintet's virtuosity, Parker's lightning-fast solo

5. "Hot House" - Composer: Tadd Dameron (1945) Anthem of the bebop movement, famously performed by Gillespie and Parker

6. "Drum Conversation" - Max Roach's impressive drum solo monologue

Other songs performed at the concert include:

- "A Night in Tunisia"
- "I've Got You Under My Skin"
- "Embraceable You"
- "Sure Thing"
- "Cherokee"
- "Hallelujah"
- "Lullaby of Birdland"

In 1995, *Jazz at Massey Hall* was inducted into the Grammy Hall of Fame.

Parker's passing in 1955 signaled the end of the bebop era, a revolution he spearheaded with his groundbreaking style. He embroidered hundreds of standard lines into his solos with clarity and cohesiveness. Parker shaped a musical language that was rhythmically vibrant, concisely expressive, and characterized by emotional depth, fluidity, and fortitude. Visionary artists like Parker leave an indelible voice, defining the beginning and end of an era. Similarly, when Johann Sebastian Bach, the musical genius architect of Western European counterpoint, died in 1750, his passing concluded the Baroque period (1600s-1750). Like Bach, Parker forged a parallel legacy, expanding American music's cultural and expressive horizons.

Through dedicated practice and commitment, Parker established a progressive oral tradition in jazz, compiled by blistering tempos, ingenious ornamentations, and improvisational virtuosity unparalleled in the performing arts. His inventive genius and vivid imagination propelled him to craft a sonic universe, distinctively weaving the lineage of Jazz music and other influences like Bartok and Stravinsky, 20th-century classical composers, in his sound. Parker's artistry redefined American music, yet skeptics continue to question bebop's artistic merit and universal appeal. Unlike Baroque, which experienced a resurgence, jazz faces ongoing criticism, underscoring the complexity of its legacy.

The Clifford Brown-Max Roach Quintet: A New Paradigm

The Jazz Quintet legacy experienced an urgent shift forward in the 1950s, as beboppers prioritized artistic integrity, nurtured rising talent, and revolutionized the sound of jazz from bebop to hard bop. The Clifford Brown-Max Roach Quintet emerged amid this transformation, redefining the trumpet and saxophone quintet sound. This trailblazing group, led by trumpet virtuoso Clifford Brown and drum legend Max Roach, represented a bold new direction. Their seminal 1954 recording, "Clifford Brown & Max Roach Quintet," remains one of the most distinctive Bop ensembles until Brown's tragic passing in 1956, at just 25 years old.

Selected Recording:

Album: *Clifford Brown-Max Roach Quintet* Release: December 1954 Studio: Capitol (Hollywood) Label: EmArcy

Artists:

- Clifford Brown: Trumpet

- Harold Land: Tenor Saxophone

- Richie Powell: Piano

- George Morrow: Bass

- Max Roach: Drums

Timeless Classics: "Joy Spring," composed by Clifford Brown, showcases the quintet's brilliance. Clifford Brown-Max Roach recordings were inducted into the 1996 Grammy Hall of Fame.

From the Creator, through the Artist, to the Audience

Art Blakey and the Jazz Messengers formed a new chapter in the jazz quintet's evolution with their 1958 masterpiece, "Moanin'." This iconic album inaugurated the hard bop movement, a variant of bebop that infused traditional gospel and blues into its improvisational core. Hard bop's distinctive sound builds upon a triplet-based groove with a high-spirited, decorative call-and-response performance technique. This hard-driving jazz style returned to the roots of Black American music and propelled the genre forward, embracing newfound freedom of expression. When performed at its highest level, hard bop music elicits a visceral response, stirring audiences to tap their feet, snap their fingers, and nod their heads in rhythm. The music becomes a soulful communal experience, with shout choruses urging soloists to soar to new heights. After each dynamic performance, Art Blakey would introduce the band members and humbly remind audiences that the music flows from the creator, through the artist, to the audience.

Selected Recording:

Album: *Moanin': Art Blakley and the Jazz Messengers.* Release Date: October 30, 1958, Studio: Van Gelder Studio, Hackensack, New Jersey Label: Blue Note (BLP4003)

Artists:

- Lee Morgan: Trumpet
- Benny Golson: Tenor Saxophone
- Bobby Timmons: Piano
- Jymie Merritt: Bass
- Art Blakey: Drums

Timeless Classics: Bobby Timmons' "Moanin" exemplifies the hard bop style, while the album showcases the rich performance tradition of the jazz quintet sound. Other noteworthy selections include Art Blakey's "The Drum Thunder Suite," Benny Golson's "Blues March," "Along Came Betty," and "Are You Real."

Art Blakey's (1919-1990) illustrious 50-year career demonstrated his innovative spirit and distinctive drumming style, deeply rooted in African influences. His playing was a masterful blend of bombast and nuance, imbued with meaning and purpose. From the stage, Blakey would often proclaim, "Music washes away the dust of everyday life," encapsulating the transformative power of his art.

The Jazz Messengers, Blakey's iconic ensemble, stood as a beacon of excellence, fostering a legacy that inspires generations. This revered collective transformed lives and served as a launching pad for some of jazz's most brilliant talents. A staggering array of Messenger alumni went on to become luminaries in their own right, including Wayne Shorter, Freddie Hubbard, Woody Shaw, Cedar Walton, Kenny Dorham, Mulgrew Miller, Benny Green, Eddie Henderson, Curtis Fuller, Kenny Garrett, Wallace Roney, James Williams, Peter Washington, Terence Blanchard, Donald Harrison, and the Marsalis brothers, among many others. These remarkable artists, along with numerous others, have contributed significantly to upholding the rich heritage of jazz. As ambassadors of American music, Art Blakey and the Jazz Messengers traversed the globe, spreading the universal language of jazz and its ability to uplift and transcend everyday struggles.

The Legend of Miles Davis

Miles Davis (1926-1991), a visionary trumpeter and relentless innovator, left a massive footprint on jazz. In the late 1950s and mid-1960s, Davis led two iconic quintets, each featuring a distinct configuration of legendary musicians. The first quintet (1955-1958) announced the coming out of John Coltrane, while the second (1964-1968) featured saxophonist Wayne Shorter, pianist Herbie Hancock, bassist Ron Carter, and drummer Tony Williams.

These two ensembles, along with the Brown-Roach Quintet and the Jazz Messengers, formed the vanguard of hard bop. In 1956, the Miles Davis Quintet recorded four seminal albums in just two days: "Relaxin'," "Workin'," "Steamin'," and "Cookin'." These sessions, reissued in 2006 as a four-disc box set, showcased the quintet's remarkable chemistry and launched the careers of its members.

The late 1950s recordings of the Miles Davis Quintet are breathtaking, with Davis's muted trumpet and Coltrane's inventive tenor saxophone weaving a spell of beauty and innovation. Davis's distinctive, muted trumpet sound and cool demeanor became his trademark for decades. His 1958 "Stella by Starlight" rendition exemplifies this signature style, influencing generations of jazz musicians.

Miles Davis was a master of contrasting styles, effortlessly shifting from lyrical balladeer to virtuosic technician. His rendition of "Half Nelson" showcases his remarkable agility, speed, and timing, with nuanced rhythmic phrasing reminiscent of his mentors, Dizzy Gillespie and Charlie Parker.

The first edition of the Miles Davis Quintet recordings is renowned for its infectious swing, driven by the rhythm section's dynamic interplay. Red Garland's elegant piano, Paul Chambers's propulsive bass, and Philly Joe Jones's explosive drums created a partnership that elevated the entire ensemble.

Artists:

- Miles Davis: Trumpet
- John Coltrane: Tenor Saxophone
- Red Garland: Piano
- Paul Chambers: Bass
- Philly Joe Jones: Drums

Timeless Classics from the Relaxin' LP:

- "Oleo," composed by Sonny Rollins
- "Woody 'N You," composed by Dizzy Gillespie

Timeless Classics from the *Workin'* LP:

- "Four," composed by Miles Davis
- "It Never Entered My Mind," composed by Richard Rodgers
- "In Your Own Sweet Way," composed by Dave Brubeck
- "Half Nelson," composed by Miles Davis
- "Ahmad's Blues," by Ahmad Jamal

Timeless Classics from the *Steamin'* LP:

- "Well You Needn't," composed by Thelonious Monk
- "When I Fall In Love," was composed by Victor Young

Timeless Classics from the *Cookin'* LP:

- "My Funny Valentine" was composed by Richard Rodgers

Other noteworthy selections from the Miles Davis Quintet:

- "Round Midnight" was composed by Thelonious Monk. Released: March 18, 1957, Label: Columbia

Creativity and Spontaneity

Miles Davis' second great quintet embarked on a revolutionary journey, exploring uncharted territories in jazz. This ensemble, featuring Wayne Shorter, Herbie Hancock, Ron Carter, and Tony Williams, delved into a more avant-garde approach while maintaining elements of the structured hard bop style that defined Davis' earlier work. He kept using the Harmon mute, and the group continued their work in jazz standards. However, the feeling of complacency began to haunt and stifle their musical expressions. The group needed to turn the corner.

The 1960s jazz landscape marked the emergence of free jazz, led by Ornette Coleman's groundbreaking explorations.

Coleman's 1960 album *Free Jazz: A Collective Improvisation* featured an unconventional double quartet, and his 1965 live recording *At The Golden Circle* Vol. 1 & 2. This album, featuring an Avant-Garde jazz trio with Ornette on Alto saxophone, trumpet, and violin, David Izenson on bass, and Charles Moffett on drums, showcased the trio's unconventional approach to what Moffett described as freedom with discipline, characterized by a rejection of traditional song forms and chord structures. But more on Ornette Coleman later.

Davis and his second quintet shared a similar penchant for innovation. Their music was a dynamic, collective exploration, navigating uncharted territories with each performance. The ensemble's improvisational approach was rooted in rhythmic, free-blowing structures, leaving ample space for creativity and spontaneity.

The Miles Davis second great quintet recorded five studio albums, including *E.S.P.* (1965), *Miles Smiles* (1966), *Sorcerer* (1967), *Nefertiti* (1968), and *Miles in the Sky* (1968). However, their live performances, as captured in the iconic *Live at the Plugged Nickel* (1965), remain the apex of their achievements.

This live album, recorded on December 22-23, 1965, *Live at the Plugged Nickel* in Chicago, showcases the quintet's remarkable chemistry and innovation. The setlist features a mix of Davis originals, including "So What," "Agitation," and "Milestone," alongside timeless standards like "Yesterdays," "If I Were a Bell," and "Stella by Starlight." The Plugged Nickel live recordings embody a captivating dichotomy of emotions: bold, innocent, vulnerable, confident, and belonging. This seminal album remains a testament to the Davis second great quintet's innovative lifeforce and enduring influence on jazz.

The Complete Live at the Plugged Nickel (1965):

Recorded Date: December 22nd & 23rd, 1965 Released Date: March 1992 Venue: Plugged Nickel Label: Sony Records (catalogue SRCS 5766-5772)

Artists:

- Miles Davis: Trumpet

- Wayne Shorter: Tenor Saxophone

- Herbie Hancock: Piano

- Ron Carter: Bass

- Tony Williams: Drums

The Horace Silver Quintet: A Legacy of Jazz Excellence

Horace Silver (1928-2014) was a creative and imaginative pianist who led one of the most influential jazz quintets of the 1950s. As a master of classic compositional design, Silver's works for trumpet and tenor saxophone are revered benchmarks of jazz excellence. His impressive discography boasts iconic masterpieces such as "Doodlin'," "Strollin'," "Tokyo Blues," "The Preacher," "Sister Sadie," "Señor Blues," "Filthy McNasty," "Nica's Dream," and "Song for My Father," solidifying his status as a master composer for ensemble in the company of artists like Monk, Shorter, Golson, Mingus, and a few others.

Silver's creative writing and playing are featured in a tall order on his 1960 album *Horace-Scope*, recorded on July 8-9 at Van Gelder Studio in Englewood Cliffs, New Jersey. This seminal work features a stellar lineup, including Blue Mitchell on trumpet, Junior Cook on tenor saxophone, Gene Taylor on bass, and Roy Brooks on drums. Together, they bring Silver's soulful compositions to life, showcasing the quintet's remarkable cohesiveness and musicianship.

Horace-Scope is a masterclass in contrapuntal composition for jazz quintet, with each track offering a unique glimpse into Silver's creative genius. From the opening notes, it's clear that this album is something special– the rhythmic precision, the soulful counterpoint between the rhythm section and the front-line instruments, gracefully demonstrating the enduring power of jazz to inspire, uplift, and transform.

The Cannonball Adderley Quintet: Soulful Hard Bop Excellence

Julian "Cannonball" Adderley (1928-1975) and his quintet revolutionized jazz with their unique blend of hard bop, gospel, and blues. Featuring Nat Adderley on cornet, Joe Zawinul on piano and Wurlitzer electric piano, Victor Gaskin on Bass, and Roy McCurdy on Drums, the group's performances often felt like a campground meeting in the Black Church. Their 1967 album, *Mercy Mercy Mercy, Live at 'The Club*, captured the essence of their soulful hard bop sound.

The album's title track, *Mercy Mercy Mercy*, penned by Joe Zawinul, became an instant classic. This bluesy composition speaks to the hardships of life, with Cannonball's poignant introduction setting the tone: "You know, sometimes we're not prepared for adversity... when it happens, we're caught short. We don't know exactly how to handle it... Sometimes we don't know what to do when adversity takes over." Cannonball's heartfelt words seamlessly transition into Zawinul's uplifting melody, showcasing the quintet's skill in crafting deeply personal and universally relatable music.

The Cannonball Adderley Quintet's *Mercy Mercy Mercy* remains an iconic anthem that is so familiar, and its heartfelt rhythms continue to inspire generations of jazz enthusiasts. This recording is yet another seminal work in the evolution of bebop, cementing the group's status as one of the most influential jazz ensembles of all time, and their music remains a timeless reflection of the human experience.

Rising Stars: Carrying the Torch of Jazz Excellence

The legacy of great quintets continued to thrive into the 1980s, with a new generation of rising stars pushing the boundaries of jazz excellence. Alto saxophonist Kenny Garrett's 1984 release, featuring trumpeter Woody Shaw, marked a significant milestone in this era. Other notable quintets emerged, including Terence Blanchard and Donald Harrison's 1987 "Crystal Stair" recording, trumpeter Wallace Roney's 1987 "Verses" LP with Gary Thomas on tenor saxophone, and trumpeter Roy Hargrove's 1990 release "Diamond in the Rough" with Alto saxophonist Antonio Hart.

Pianist Marcus Roberts' 1989 LP *The Truth Is Spoken Here* further demonstrated the depth of talent among these rising stars. The Wynton Marsalis Group, featuring Branford Marsalis on saxophones, Kenny Kirkland on piano, Jeff "Tain" Watts on drums, and Charnett Moffett on bass, reached new heights with their 1985 recording "Black Codes (from the Underground)." This masterpiece earned the group a Grammy Award for Best Jazz Instrumental Performance– group, marking Wynton Marsalis' arrival not only as a great trumpeter but also as a gifted composer.

The "Black Codes" recording is a landmark album, with a swing that has no parallel in the 1980s era. Its legendary status in the annals of jazz history is well-deserved, cementing the Wynton Marsalis Group's footprint as one of the most influential jazz ensembles of their time.

As we reflect on the impact of Bebop on the jazz landscape, it becomes clear that this revolutionary movement was more than just a musical phenomenon– it was a cultural and social watershed moment that continues to reverberate through the corridors of American history. Emerging in the 1940s, Bebop not only transformed the jazz idiom but also played a pivotal role in shaping the cultural and social fabric of the nation. As a powerful symbol of Black American creativity and resistance, Bebop helped to challenge the racist stereotypes and social injustices that pervaded American society during this tumultuous era.

The Bebop movement, emphasizing virtuosity, complexity, and improvisation, not only raised the bar for jazz musicians but also helped create a new cultural paradigm that celebrated innovation, experimentation, and creative expression. As a result, Bebop inspired a generation of young Black American musicians who sought to challenge the status quo and push the boundaries of artistic expression. The likes of Charlie Parker, Dizzy Gillespie, Thelonious Monk, and Kenny Clarke, among others, became icons of this movement, washing away the dust of life and leaving their footprints on the heart and soul of humanity.

CHAPTER NINE

THE COOL JAZZ EXPERIENCE: A TALE OF TWO STORIES
(1950-1960)

The 1950s witnessed the emergence of Cool Jazz, a dominant style that followed the bebop movement of the 1940s. Despite bebop innovations and the nascent hard bop style, Cool Jazz carved out a unique space with less tension and a more relaxed musical expression. This style was the antithesis of bebop, with its fast tempos, harmonic sophistication, and rhythmic complexity.

The cultural landscape of the 1950s was marked by a heightened awareness of racial and cultural appropriation in Black American music genres. With their intense, radical advocacy of social justice and musical integrity, Bebop musicians represented a cultural renaissance of Blackness. In contrast, the Cool Jazz movement, emphasizing easy living, simplicity, and colorful arrangements, aligned with the West Coast Jazz aesthetic. Large ensembles, orchestral underpinnings, and non-traditional jazz instruments such as the bassoon, oboe, French horn, and flute characterized this style.

The Cool Jazz movement experienced a resurgence of musicians of European descent in prominent roles, including trumpeter Chet Baker, pianist-composer Lennie Tristano, and alto saxophonist Paul Desmond. However, the visionary pioneers of this style were Miles Davis and Gil Evans, who collaborated on a series of seminal recordings that redefined the jazz landscape.

Gil Evans, a Canadian-born arranger and composer, honed his skills in California before moving to New York City, where he collaborated with Miles Davis on a series of orchestrations for a nonet, instrumentation comprised of French horns, trombones, and tubas. This collaboration signaled a significant shift from the quintet ensembles that dominated the bebop era and a radical departure from the traditional jazz ensemble.

The collaboration between Miles Davis and Gil Evans resulted in four seminal recordings representing Cool Jazz's apotheosis. These albums, including *Birth of the Cool*, *Miles Ahead*, *Porgy and Bess*, and *Sketches of Spain*, showcased the duo's innovative and visionary approach to jazz, which emphasized subtle shifts in harmony, tempo, and timbre.

The *Birth of the Cool* recording sessions, which took place in 1949 and 1950, featured a nonet ensemble that included Lee Konitz, Gerry Mulligan, Bill Barber, and other key personnel contributors. The album's release in February 1957 marked an effervescent footprint in post-bebop development, introducing a unique harmonic conception, slow tempos, and a lower brass mid-range sonic design. Inescapably, the Cool Jazz movement, exemplified by the collaboration between Miles Davis and Gil Evans, represented the most significant departure from the mainstream of Jazz music.

Birth of the Cool Personnel

- Trumpet – Miles Davis
- Alto Saxophone – Lee Konitz
- Baritone Saxophone – Gerry Mulligan
- French Horn – Junior Collins/Gunther Schuller/Sandy Siegelstein
- Trombone – Kai Winding/J.J. Johnson/Mike Zwerin
- Tuba – Bill Barber
- Piano – Al Haig/John Lewis
- Bass – Joe Shulman/Nelson Boyd/Al McKibbon
- Drums – Max Roach/Kenny Clarke

Miles Davis and Gil Evans' second collaborative masterpiece, *Miles Ahead*, was a vanguard experience showcasing Cool Jazz's essence. Recorded in five sessions between May and August 1957, and released in October of the same year, this exemplary album featured a nineteen-piece jazz orchestra. As a paragon of sophistication, *Miles Ahead* embodies the apogee of jazz refinement, elegantly expanding on the traditions of its predecessors.

Indeed, this poetic recording is a suite of emotions, weaving a complex narrative that tells two stories simultaneously. Miles Davis, the protagonist and antagonist, masterfully crafts a single, cohesive tale that conveys his imaginative style and innovative approach to jazz. Through *Miles Ahead*, Davis and Evans pushed the boundaries of Cool Jazz, creating a work that remains a landmark in the genre.

Miles Davis and Gil Evans' third collaborative masterpiece, *Porgy and Bess* was a groundbreaking jazz orchestration of George Gershwin's 1935 folk opera. This iconic work held great historical significance, particularly in its original production, which featured civil rights activist Robert Todd Duncan (1912-1998) as the pioneering "Porgy." A Simmons University (HBCU) alumnus in Louisville, Kentucky, Duncan fearlessly broke the color barrier in theater, defying the racist norms that forced African Americans to use side entrances and sit in segregated balconies.

Duncan's co-star, Anne Wiggins Brown (1912-2009), who portrayed "Bess," was another trailblazing artist. A Morgan College (HBCU) alumnus in Baltimore, Maryland, Brown's singing of the composition "Summertime" convinced Gershwin to change the opera's title to "Porgy and Bess," reflecting the importance of her role. After being rejected from Peabody Institute for her race, Brown became the first African American vocalist admitted to the Juilliard School of Music in 1928. Her remarkable journey and Duncan's paved the way for Miles Davis and Gil Evans to reimagine Gershwin's masterpiece.

In the summer of 1958, Davis and Evans embarked on four recording sessions, culminating in the March 1959 release of "Porgy and Bess." This seminal work expanded the historical narrative of jazz, illuminating its impact on American culture. The 1959 release of Gershwin's original 1935 Broadway production exhibited Davis and Evans' vision of a cinematic masterpiece, seamlessly blending melody, lyricism, and modal improvisation. The *Porgy and Bess* recording remains a momentous accomplishment in African American literature and culture in the 20th century.

Miles Davis and Gil Evans' fourth collaborative masterpiece, *Sketches of Spain,* represented an expansion of jazz music's emotional and cultural milieu. Building on the success of Davis' groundbreaking modal classic, "Kind of Blue," this 1960 project flawlessly wove together elements of Spanish folk tradition, classical music, and jazz. Recorded in three sessions between November 1959 and March 1960, and released in July 1960, *Sketches of Spain* transcended genre boundaries, embedding itself into the very fabric of world music. The result is a work of sublime beauty that continues to enthrall listeners to this day.

The album's centerpiece, *Concierto de Aranjuez*, a 20th-century contemporary Spanish composition by Joaquín Rodrigo, is reimagined through Evans' interpretive orchestrations and Davis' poignant trumpet sketches. This hauntingly beautiful performance is a robust synthesis of different cultures and traditions, creating a timeless, influential masterwork that continues to inspire musicians across genres.

Miles Ahead, Porgy and Bess, and *Sketches of Spain* Personnel:

- Miles Davis – Trumpet, flugelhorn
- Bernie Glow – Lead trumpet
- Ernie Royal – Trumpet
- Louis Mucci – Trumpet

- Taft Jordan – Trumpet
- John Carisi – Trumpet (Miles Ahead, Porgy and Bess only)
- Johnny Coles – Trumpet (Porgy and Bess, Sketches of Spain only)
- Joe Bennett – Trombone
- Jimmy Cleveland – Trombone
- Frank Rehak – Trombone
- Dick Hixon – Trombone (Porgy and Bess, Sketches of Spain only)
- Tom Mitchell – Bass trombone (Miles Ahead only)
- Willie Ruff – French horn (Miles Ahead, Porgy and Bess only)
- Jim Buffington – French horn (Miles Ahead, Sketches of Spain only)
- Tony Miranda – French horn (Miles Ahead, Sketches of Spain only)
- Julius Watkins – French horn (Porgy and Bess only)
- Gunther Schuller – French horn (Porgy and Bess only)
- John Barrows – French horn (Sketches of Spain only)
- James Buffington – French Horn (Sketches of Spain only)
- Earl Chapin – French Horn (Sketches of Spain only)
- Joe Singer – French horn (Sketches of Spain only)
- Bill Barber – Sousaphone
- Jimmy McAllister – Sousaphone (Sketches of Spain only)
- Lee Konitz – Alto saxophone (Miles Ahead only)
- Cannonball Adderley – Alto saxophone (Porgy and Bess only)
- Danny Bank – Bass clarinet, alto flute, bass flute
- Sid Cooper – Flute and clarinet (Miles Ahead only)
- Albert Block – Flute (Sketches of Spain only)

- Eddie Caine – Flute (Sketches of Spain only)

- Harold Feldman – Flute, oboe, clarinet (Sketches of Spain only)

- Romeo Penque – Oboe (Sketches of Spain only)

- Jack Knitzer – Bassoon (Sketches of Spain only)

- Paul Chambers – Double bass

- Art Taylor – Drums (Miles Ahead only)

- Philly Joe Jones – Drums (Porgy and Bess only)

- Jimmy Cobb – Drums (Porgy and Bess, Sketches of Spain only)

- Elvin Jones – Percussion (Sketches of Spain only)

- Elden "Buster" Bailey – Percussion (Sketches of Spain only)

- José Mangual Sr. – Castanets (Sketches of Spain only)

- Wynton Kelly – Piano (Miles Ahead, Porgy and Bess only)

- Janet Putnam – Harp (Sketches of Spain only)

- Gil Evans – Arranger and Conductor

Undeniably, the Cool Jazz Experience was a catalytic movement that redefined the jazz arena and reflected the complexities of American society in the 1950s. The tale of two stories– one of innovation and creativity, the other of social and cultural tension– is a monument to the power of jazz to capture the zeitgeist of its time. Through the works of Miles Davis, Gil Evans, and other visionary musicians, Cool Jazz embodied the spirit of relaxation, simplicity, and elegance, providing a refreshing contrast to the intensity of bebop.

As we reflect on the significance of Cool Jazz, it becomes clear that this movement was not just a musical phenomenon, but a cultural and social commentary on the America of its time. The collaborations between Miles Davis and Gil Evans, in particular, represented a new paradigm in jazz that emphasized harmony, texture, and mood. Their iconic recordings, such as "Birth of the Cool," "Miles Ahead," "Porgy and Bess," "Sketches of Spain," and "Kind of Blue," continue to inspire generations of musicians and music enthusiasts, offering a timeless glimpse into the creative genius of the Cool Jazz era.

In conclusion, The Cool Jazz Experience was a pivotal moment in the evolution of jazz, one that not only reflected the complexities of American society but also helped to shape the course of jazz history. Looking back on this era, the power of jazz transcends boundaries, innovates, and inspires. The legacy of Cool Jazz continues to resonate with us today, testifying to the enduring spirit of creativity and innovation that defines America's greatest musical art form.

CHAPTER TEN

AVANT-GARDE: A FREE JAZZ MOVEMENT

(1960-1980)

The 1960s were a transformative decade that changed the world forever. The first American spacewalk occurred in June of 1965, followed by Neil Armstrong's historic moon landing on July 21, 1969. This monumental achievement marked a giant leap forward in human exploration and creativity.

The 1960s also witnessed the birth of the Free Jazz movement, a kindling that ignited an explosive firestorm of creativity and innovation. Free Jazz artists improvised without adhering to fixed structures, meters, tempos, or predetermined chord progressions, expressing themselves in various dimensions, including theatrical, visual, experimental, and spiritual. These artists may disregard the physical or concrete existence of melody and harmony altogether, focusing more on creative ways to present abstract conceptions such as love, beauty, equality, and freedom.

Avant-Garde Free Jazz artists subscribed to a political, psychological, cultural, and historical reassessment and redefinition of Eurocentric assumptions of Black identity. These musicians, many of whom were also music professors in higher education, pushed the boundaries of Jazz performance and challenged traditional notions of music and art. Music pioneers Eric Dolphy, Albert Ayler, Cecil Taylor, Sun Ra, Archie Shepp, Don Cherry, Charlie Mingus, Alice Coltrane, the Art Ensemble of Chicago, and the Charles Moffett Family Jazz Band were at the forefront of this movement.

The 1960s Free Jazz movement built upon a rich musical heritage spanning centuries. From the emergence of Ma Rainey, the mother of the blues, to the flowering of art with the arrival of bebop, jazz has always been a powerful force for creativity and resistance. Louis Armstrong, Duke Ellington, and Charlie Parker paved the way for future jazz musicians.

In the turbulent 1960s, jazz artists embarked on a movement that crystallized a soundtrack for civil rights, championed by revolutionary Black artists and intellectuals of the era. The overarching epoch of events that birthed a musical cacophony included Black students' sit-in demonstrations against segregated lunch counters, the assassinations of John and Robert Kennedy, Malcolm X, Martin Luther King Jr., and the increased U.S. involvement in the Vietnam War, testifying to a crossroad crisis and a radical call for change.

In an environment of massive anti-war protests in America, Nobel Peace Prize laureate and civil rights drum major for justice, Rev. Dr. Martin Luther King, Jr., asked a probing question in his book, *Where Do We Go from Here: Chaos or Community?* Jazz masters John Coltrane, Ornette Coleman, Pharoah Sanders, and Max Roach were prophetic voices who provided hope for a better future. Similarly, Soul music artists like James Brown, Sam Cooke, and Aretha Franklin, as well as Gospel music artists like The Staple Singers, Mahalia Jackson, and Donny Hathaway, responded with a call to action.

Duke Ellington, Sonny Greer, 1946 @ the Aquarium, NYC

Where Do We Go From Here: Chaos or Community?

In February of 1960, John Coltrane released his iconic album *Giant Steps*, which consisted solely of his original works. This album is a monumental achievement that pushed the boundaries of harmonic complexity and technical ability. Coltrane's clear direction, fully displayed as *Giant Steps*, offers a benchmark for individual and collective discipline. The composition is one of the most challenging pieces to improvise in jazz, raising the bar for those committed to being a force for good. *Giant Steps* has been extensively analyzed and studied in music conservatories worldwide, cementing its place as a pinnacle of excellence in jazz.

Personnel:

- John Coltrane - Tenor saxophone
- Tommy Flanagan – Piano
- Paul Chambers - Bass
- Art Taylor – Drums

Lionel Hampton, 1946, Aquarium, NYC

Change of the Century: Composed by Ornette Coleman

Ornette Coleman (1930-2015), the father of Free Jazz, released *Change of the Century* in May 1960, reflecting the radical shift in style that departed from conventional jazz norms. This album marked a new era in the genre, much like the start of a new century represents a significant change in time. The title *Change of the Century* signified a major historical transition, and the recording aligned with this theme, featuring Coleman's compositional originality, creative improvisations, provocative melodic motifs, layered and overlapping group dialogue, and a driving rhythm section.

Ornette Coleman and his piano-less quartet challenged listeners to abandon their preconceptions. The personnel included Ornette Coleman on Alto saxophone, Don Cherry on pocket trumpet, Charlie Haden on bass, and Billy Higgins on Drums.

In September 1961, Coleman recorded *Free Jazz: A Collective Improvisation,* a continuous 37-minute free improvisation. This album brought a more aggressive, cacophonous texture to Coleman's work and coined "free jazz" for a new development in jazz music. However, Coleman's radical ideas provoked antagonism and resentment from many of his contemporaries.

Upon arriving in New York in the late 1950s, Coleman was viewed as a nonconformist and criticized harshly for abandoning the status quo. His musical theory, which he referred to as "harmolodics," represented a new way of thinking about music, giving equal value to harmony, melody, and rhythm while disregarding conventional key and time signatures.

Coleman defined his harmolodic theory as "the use of the physical and mental logic of one's own making, expressed in sound." Some musicians who worked with Coleman referred to his concept as a continuous state of modulation. Renowned bassist Charnett Moffett, whose first name is a combination of

Charles Moffett and Ornette Coleman, after an intense rehearsal with Coleman and many years of close family relations, pronounced the critical concept of Ornette's music is to improvise in all twelve keys simultaneously in the moment.

In this way, the harmolodic approach involves creating a complex sound by layering notes and poly-tonalities from different keys on each other, unrestrained by tonal limitations, rhythmic pre-determinations, or harmonic rules. The harmolodic idea is a relentless universal pursuit of freedom and liberation. Ornette Coleman's Double Quartet, featuring Ornette on alto saxophone, Eric Dolphy on bass clarinet, Don Cherry on pocket trumpet, Freddie Hubbard on trumpet, Charlie Haden on bass, Scott LaFaro on bass, Billy Higgins on drums, and Ed Blackwell on drums, showcased Coleman's harmolodic theory in action.

Freedom Day

"Freedom Day," the second track on Max Roach's seminal 1960 album *We Insist: Freedom Now Suite*, verifies the drummer's innovative spirit and commitment to social justice. This brilliant album, featuring all original compositions, is a masterclass in Avant-Garde Free Jazz musical design and destination. Max Roach's personnel include Oscar Brown Jr. - Lyricist, Abbey Lincoln - vocalist, Booker Little - trumpet, Julian Priester - trombone, Coleman Hawkins and Walter Benton - tenor saxophone, James Schenk - bass, Raymond Mantilla, Tomas du Vall, and Michael Olatunji - congas.

On this recording, Abbey Lincoln's sublime vocals and Oscar Brown Jr.'s poignant lyrics converge in a masterpiece of collaborative artistry, evoking a sense of flawless creation.

Released in December 1960, *We Insist!* is a vocal-instrumental suite that tackles themes related to the civil rights movement. Through compositions like "Driva Man," "Freedom Day," "Triptych: Prayer, Protest, Peace," "All Africa," and

"Tears for Johannesburg," Max Roach tells a story of civil rights struggles, emancipation, brutality, determination, oppression, rage, and peacefulness.

This album's aspirations were fueled by the protest sit-ins at the Woolworth department store lunch counter in Greensboro, North Carolina, and the momentum of the civil rights movement. With "We Insist!", Max Roach created a landmark album that continues to inspire and educate listeners about the power of music as a force for social change.

We Insist! " is reminiscent of African American folk music aesthetics, evoking the spirit of protest and resistance. One of the album's most striking compositions is "Driva' Man," a haunting personification of the white overseer in slavery times who exploited and abused women under his jurisdiction. The musical theme is rooted in a C minor pentatonic scale, composed in an unconventional six-measure blues structure in 5/4-time meter. The lyrics of "Driva' Man" paint a vivid picture of life under oppression:

Driva' man he made a life

But the Mamie ain't his wife

Choppin' cotton, don't be slow

Better finish out your row

Keep a-movin' with that plow

Driva' man'll show ya how

You get to work and root that stump

Driva' man'll make ya jump

Better make your hammer ring

Driva' man'll start to swing

Ain't but two things on my mind

Driva' man quittin' time

Driva'man de kind of boss

Ride a man and lead a horse

When his cat'o nine tail fly

You'd be happy just to die

Runaway and you'll be found

By his big old red bone hound

Peter oller bring your back

Make you sorry you is Black

Driva'man he made a life

But the Mamie ain't his wife

Ain't but two things on my mind

Driva'man quittin' time

These poignant lyrics capture the brutality and inhumanity of slavery, while also conveying the resilience and determination of those who endured it. Through "Driva' Man" and the rest of the "We Insist!" album, Max Roach and his collaborators created a powerful and enduring testament to the struggle for freedom and human dignity.

Alabama: A Musical Elegy for a Nation in Turmoil

John Coltrane's poignant musical elegy entitled *Alabama* was inspired by the devastating September 1963 bombing of the 16th Street Baptist Church in Birmingham, Alabama. This tragic event claimed the lives of four innocent Black girls - Addie Mae Collins, Cynthia Wesley, Carole Robertson, and Carol Denise McNair – and sparked widespread civil unrest.

Coltrane's heartfelt composition, recorded in November 1963 and featured on his 1964 album "Live at Birdland," was a powerful tribute to the victims and a call to action for human rights and civil rights in America. The musical expressions were communal and solemn, comforting the souls of the American people.

Based on the eulogy Dr. Martin Luther King Jr. delivered, Coltrane's "Alabama" captured the mood and sentiment of a grieving community. This iconic composition validates the significance and vital role of the Avant-Garde Free Jazz movement.

Musically, "Alabama" is a soft, mournful cry played in C minor pentatonic mode, with rolling thunder colorations from the rhythm section. Coltrane's free-form rubato pedal tone magnifies pain, grief, and anger in response to racial injustice. The personnel on this recording include pianist McCoy Tyner, bassist Jimmy Garrison, and drummer Elvin Jones.

Pharoah Sanders Spiritual Expressions: *Journey to the One*

Pharoah Sanders (1940-2022) was a visionary saxophonist who revolutionized jazz with his innovative, multi-phonic performance techniques. His towering tenor saxophone playing was an expression of spirituality, punctuated by ecstatic shouts, screams, and expressions of praise.

Deeply influenced by Ornette Coleman's "Free Jazz" movement, Sanders collaborated extensively with John Coltrane on Impulse! recording productions, including *Ascension, Meditation, Om*, and *A Love Supreme: Live in Seattle*. These groundbreaking collaborations, from 1965 to 1967, showcased Sanders' unique voice and style.

Sanders' seminal free jazz album *Journey to the One* crystallized his musical vision, revealing insightful inner convictions and a deep concern for humanity. His discography includes other notable works, such as "The Creator Has a

Master Plan," "Morning Prayer," "The Gathering," "Black Unity," "Love Is Everywhere," "Love Will Find a Way," and "You've Got to Have Freedom."

Soul Music

Amid massive anti-war protests and civil unrest in America, two revolutionary musical movements emerged: Free Jazz and Soul Music. While Jazz artists like Ornette Coleman and John Coltrane pioneered the liberating language of Free Jazz, Rhythm and Blues artists like Aretha Franklin, James Brown, Stevie Wonder, and Sam Cooke crafted a new musical expression that captured the essence of Soul Music.

These two diverse performance traditions worked in tandem, reflecting the turbulent times and the quest for freedom and equality. Soul music artists, in particular, embodied a deep philosophical and poetic aesthetic, conveying a message of resolve and defiance in the face of persistent oppression. From the civil rights anthems of James Brown's "Say it Loud - I'm Black and Proud" to Sam Cooke's "A Change is Gonna Come," Soul music artists delivered a powerful message of perseverance and determination, proclaiming, *We've made up our minds, we won't turn around, we're freedom-bound.*

We've Made Up Our Minds, We Won't Turn Around, We're Freedom-Bound

Singer-songwriter Stevie Wonder's album "Songs in the Key of Life." Tells a compelling story about love for America against conflicts of strife. The album celebrates personal triumph over despair and a call for peace and universal prayer. In Wonder's opening song, *"Love's in Need of Love Today,"* he cautions all to, "Don't delay, send yours in right away." Poetically expressed, I, too, offer an arts-based historical portrait of the soul music era of Wonder's time:

141

The great Staple Singers stood bravely on the front lines, with their soulful voices

at play

Singing out against injustice, "Marching Up Freedom's Highway,"

Inspired by Dr. King's message of equality

Protecting people from hate and bigotry

The great Ray Charles, known as the piano genius, and father of soul

Blowing alto saxophone in an improvising role

Swinging the beat with his bebop lines

Writing visionary songs, confessing "Hard Times"

"We've Got Some Difficult Days Ahead,"

Courageous Martin Luther King professed,

Walking in the footsteps of our ancestors -

To an unknown freedom address.

With faith, the substance of things hoped for,

The great Mahalia Jackson humming and leading the way

We'll "Move On Up A Little Higher"

To be free one day

Remember John Coltrane, courageous saxophone king,

Turned his sorrow chant into "A Love Supreme," "A Love Supreme"

Walking hand-in-hand, heart-to-heart,

We won't turn round, we're freedom-bound!

With perseverance and determination

We won't turn round, we're freedom-bound.

Remember Billie Holiday's "Strange Fruit,"

With blood on the leaves and blood at the root

Southern trees bear "Strange Fruit"

The Queen of Soul Aretha Franklin and trailblazer Nina Simone

Both famous for singing this song

"Young, Gifted, and Black," so be encouraged

Your Soul's intact

The great Marvin Gaye's song of songs

"Save the Children," and "What's Going On"

Freedom and justice is what we treasure

We must all take a precautionary measure

Remember Soul legend Donny Hathaway

"For All We Know," it was all a dream

Forever keep your self-respect and your pride

Get yourself in gear, keep your stride

Never mind your fears, brighter days will soon be here

Take it from me

"Someday we'll all be free"

"We've made up our minds, we won't turn round, we're freedom-bound."

As the curtains close on this exploration of the Avant-Garde Free Jazz Movement, an appreciation for the innovative spirit, creative genius, and unwavering commitment to social justice is left defined by this pivotal moment in American cultural history. The movement's emphasis on experimentation, improvisation, and pushing the boundaries of traditional jazz idioms expanded the possibilities of musical expression and mirrored the tumultuous social and cultural landscape of the 1960s.

Billie Holiday, 1947, Downbeat Magazine

The significance of Free Jazz and Soul Music during this era cannot be overstated. These genres served as a powerful vehicle for social commentary, protest, and activism, providing a voice for the voiceless and a platform for marginalized communities to express their desires, fears, and aspirations. The iconic figures of this movement– from Ornette Coleman and John Coltrane to Sam Cooke, Aretha Franklin, and Marvin Gaye– left a huge footprint on American society, inspiring generations of artists, activists, and social justice advocates to follow in their footsteps.

As we reflect on the enduring legacy of the Avant-Garde Free Jazz Movement, the struggle for freedom, equality, and social justice remains ongoing. The movement's emphasis on creative experimentation, community empowerment, and radical social critique continues to resonate with contemporary social justice movements, from Black Lives Matter to #MeToo. We need serious musicians to continue their call as artists with integrity and musical discipline. As we move forward, we must continue to draw inspiration from the courageous visionaries of this movement, embracing their spirit of innovation and creative freedom.

Ultimately, the Avant-Garde Free Jazz Movement helped shape our understanding of the world, challenged social norms, and inspired collective action. As we celebrate the movement's enduring legacy, we honor the unsung musicians who dared to challenge the status quo, push the boundaries of creative expression, and fight for a more just and equitable societal voice. Their music, message, and unwavering commitment to jazz music at the highest level resonate with us today, inspiring us to strive for a brighter, more compassionate future.

CHAPTER ELEVEN

IMPROVISATION THROUGH THE LENS OF JAZZ MUSIC

(1980 – 21ST CENTURY)

The improvisational components of jazz music, drawing upon African oral traditions, should be a requirement in the American classroom. The vision includes a comprehensive program designed to teach entry-level students how to improvise, encapsulating the essence of jazz with its deep African roots. This program, structured around a seven-point instructional blueprint, integrates the distinct elements of jazz influenced by African derivatives. Each point, carefully crafted to build upon the last, ensures a holistic and immersive learning experience for students starting on their journey into jazz improvisation.

The Seven-Point Instructional Blueprint

The following seven-point instructional blueprint is designed to facilitate entry-level students in learning the art of jazz improvisation:

1. **Weekly Listening Focus:**

    Objective: Cultivate critical thinking and critical listening skills centered around jazz improvisation.

    Implementation: Students will learn fragments of a selected jazz solo each week. Instructors will discuss the musical sound and social and historical contexts. Recite/clap the rhythm that comprises the melody.

2. **Integrating Listening in Daily Routine:**

   Objective: Make listening an integral part of students' daily activities.

   Implementation: Develop a strategic plan devoted to listening to the sound of various jazz styles. Familiarize students with compositions that are a vital part of the musical repertoire of jazz musicians.

3. **Exposure to Live Performances:**

   Objective: Motivate and inspire students through the direct communal experience of a live jazz performance.

   Implementation: Establish routine participation in jazz performances and/or jam sessions.

4. **Learn melodies from jazz standards and jazz originals:**

   Objective: learn melodies from recordings and not from written music manuscripts.

   Implementation: Select three compositions to learn; memorize the melody for each composition until mastery of pitch and sound. Advanced players may practice transposition of each melody in all 12 keys.

5. **Explore Jazz from the historical underpinnings of Congo Square:**

   Objective: Discuss and analyze the cultural melding of jazz music in New Orleans.

Implementation: Describe the historical narrative of Congo Square, highlighting the diverse cultural influences that trace back to West African music traditions.

6. **Recreate the West African sacred dance ritual known as the "ring shout."**

Objective: Create a repository of musical works composed of Negro Spirituals, field hollers, and work songs.

Implementation: Assemble a " ring-shout" dance movement based on the Pentecostal beat; select a sacred song or perhaps an improvised call-and-response Field Holler to accompany the dance.

7. **Jazz Improvisation**

Objective: Develop improvisational skills through four (4) bars of rhythmic/melodic rhyme schemes.

Implementation: Perform a rhyme scheme utilizing the tambourine and the Pentecostal beat.

By implementing this seven-point blueprint, we can offer students a comprehensive and immersive learning experience that teaches the techniques of jazz improvisational performance and connects to its historical and cultural roots. These seven educational modules encourage arts students to understand and appreciate jazz music as a musical genre, a living history of storytelling, and a creative expression deeply rooted in the authenticity and evolution of jazz improvisation.

For several decades, I have sought firsthand insights on jazz fundamentals from accomplished musicians further to enhance a new curricula approach for teaching jazz. During my recent interviews with several jazz artists, notable reflections emerged, particularly from Branford Marsalis, a distinguished composer and National Endowment for the Arts jazz master of the tenor, alto, and soprano saxophones.

Branford Marsalis shared with me that his proficiency in jazz music developed primarily through listening to and internalizing the "sound" in jazz recordings. I asked Branford what the difference would be between sound and vocabulary. Branford responded:

> "Let's say you have an English professor who knows every word in the dictionary, and then you put him on the stage to do Shakespeare, or you took him and just put him in the pulpit, and everybody staring at him waiting for him to give a stirring sermon; How is he going to fare? It's not very good because it isn't enough just to know the words. You must know how to deliver the words with a sound relative to the period. Sound creates the delivery. The thing that moves people. What makes instrumental music great is that the sound of an instrument can have an emotional effect on a listener. Data is just Data. What is great is settling on the ideas that, as a group, we need to work on the sound. Sad songs need to sound sad, and happy songs need to sound happy. Funny songs need to sound funny. It's like a real simple premise, but that's the hardest thing to do. It took a decade to learn how to do that. Maybe more than a decade to learn how to create emotion through sound."

Further, I asked Branford to play a game of fill-in-the-blank.

Me: A student learning to play jazz must...? _____

Branford's Response: Listen to hundreds of recordings, but only about two or three records a year.

Question: In your view, name five of the most influential musicians in jazz history.

Response: That's impossible to do. I have 25; the body of work is too vast. Louis Armstrong (clearly); Sidney Bechet, Lester Young, Jelly Roll Morton, John Coltrane, and many more. Just five is crazy, even to try to name.

The jazz legacy of Black American music now represents a standard of excellence in American culture that the educational systems in urban America would do well to model. Embracing this rich heritage in and out of classrooms not only enhances the cultural literacy of our citizens but also honors a narrative of resilience, creativity, and transformation. By integrating jazz into the curriculum, we provide students with a dynamic and interpretative lens through which to view music and social history.

This new paradigm for teaching jazz music, based on critical listening, experiencing live performances, understanding cultural roots, and engaging in communal musical activities, promises to cultivate skilled musicians and enlightened individuals who appreciate the core values embedded in the jazz tradition. Through an authentic educational approach, jazz will continue to uplift and resonate across community lines, serving as a bridge between cultures worldwide.

As we bring our odyssey through "Black Music Footprints" to a triumphant close, we are left with a reverence for the transformative power of music to shape our understanding of ourselves, our communities, and our place in the world. Like a rich tapestry woven from threads of joy and sorrow, struggle and triumph, Black American music has been the soundtrack of America's conscience, echoing the hopes and fears, and the dreams and despairs of a people who have consistently used music as a means of survival, resistance, and celebration.

Through the lens of iconic figures like Scott Joplin, Louis Armstrong, Duke Ellington, Billie Holiday, and Charlie Parker, we've seen how Black American music has consistently pushed the boundaries of artistic expression, social commentary, and cultural innovation. Each genre has contributed to a narrative of creativity, ingenuity, and empowerment, from the blues' emotional intensity to jazz's improvisational genius.

Dear readers, as we lift our voices in celebration of life, love, liberty, and legacy, let's continue to honor the global footprint of Black music on American culture.

BAM!

GLOSSARY

a cappella: a style of music performed by a group of singers or a solo singer without instrumental accompaniment.

African American Experience: encompasses the diverse and often challenging narratives of individuals of African descent in the United States, shaped by a history of slavery, segregation, and ongoing struggles for civil rights and equality. These experiences have evolved significantly from the period of slavery through Reconstruction and into the Jim Crow era, reflecting both resilience and resistance against systemic oppression.

African American Music: a matrix of expressions by and about Black people in the United States of America. African American music is a collection of stories told by individuals through the phenomenon of sound and the tools of melody, harmony, and rhythm. African American music, recognized for its aesthetic currency, is a rich tradition of performance practice and exemplary integration of social critique, political commentary, and spiritual invocation.

African Music: rhythm-based, with heavy use of percussion instruments, microtones, polyrhythms, polyphonic harmonies, call-and-response, and improvisation at its core.

African Roots: refers to a person or group's ancestral lineage and cultural heritage that traces back to the African continent.

Afro-Cuban Jazz: a style that combines rhythms and instruments from Cuba and the Spanish Caribbean, developed in New York City in the 1940s.

American Culture: a combination of values, behaviors, and customs unique to the United States based upon individualism, equality, freedom, and hard work, which are all considered cultural values of America.

American Music: a melting pot of cultural influences, blending European, African, Native American, and other traditions. This fusion has led to innovative genres like jazz, blues, and rock, each characterized by unique rhythms, harmonies, and expressive styles.

Ancestors: a person's ethnic origin or descent, "roots" or heritage, or the place of birth of the person, the person's parents, or the people from whom one descended before they arrived in the United States.

Architecture of Music: the underlying structure and organization of musical pieces.

Artists: a person who creates, performs, or records music. They may also be known as musicians.

Bebop: a jazz style that Black Americans created in the 1940s.

Black American Music: a broad term often used interchangeably with African American music, encompassing many genres and styles of music that originated in Black communities and have evolved.

Blues Music: An African American musical genre that originated in the American South in the 1860s. A call-and-response pattern, the blues scale, and specific chord progressions characterize it. Blues music reflected the physical, mundane universe of African Americans.

Blue Notes: a musical note played slightly bent lower than its standard pitch to add a "blue" quality to the melody.

Bomb: a jazz term representing a pronounced accent played by the drummer.

Boogie-Woogie Blues: a style associated with the piano.

Brazilian Music: a rich and diverse collection of styles such as samba, bossa nova, choro, and others that reflect the country's culture and identity.

Cakewalk: is a dance that originated with enslaved African Americans in the Southern United States.

Call-and-response: a performance technique that consists of a musical statement given by a leader immediately followed by a response from a chorus or other participant.

Chorus: a section of a song that repeats at least twice and conveys the song's primary message.

Civil Rights Movement: a decade-long struggle by African Americans to end legalized racial discrimination and gain equal rights under the law, notably during the 1950s and 1960s.

Collective Memory: refers to the social process by which Black Americans reconstruct and share their past, fostering a shared sense of identity through the communal recall and reinterpretation of historical events. The concept of collective memory is significant in shaping Black American identity.

Collective Improvisation: simultaneous improvisation by all members of a group.

Cool Jazz: The dominant jazz style of the 1950s, led by Miles Davis.

Communal Ethos: is a set of shared values, beliefs, and practices that characterize a community.

Congo Square: a large field in New Orleans where the enslaved were allowed to gather on Sunday to sing, dance, and play their drums in their traditional manner. Congo Square remains a historical and cultural landmark in New Orleans.

Country Western Music: a popular American music style that originated in the South and West rural areas in the early 20th century. It's also known as country music.

Creole: a person who has both French, Spanish, and African ancestry and was born in the New World. Also known as "Creole of Color."

Cross-Rhythms: the interplay of contrasting rhythmic patterns.

Critical Listening: active listening, evaluating the message, and forming an analysis.

Cultural Literacy: is the ability to understand and participate in a culture's traditions, values, and activities. It also means being able to communicate effectively with people from different cultures.

Curriculum: collective engagement that utilizes diverse modules of discourse and communal involvement.

Descendant: a person who descended from a particular ancestor.

Dialogue: conversation between two or more people.

Diaspora: the dispersion of a people from their original homeland.

Dixieland Style: Chicago combo style that was prominent during the 1920s.

Emancipation Proclamation: an executive order issued by President Abraham Lincoln in 1863 that declared the freedom of all enslaved Black Americans in Confederate-held territory. The 13th Amendment was ratified in 1865, leading to the official abolition of slavery in America.

European: relating to Europe or its people.

Enslaved Africans: people who were forcibly taken from their homes in Africa and sold into slavery.

Free Jazz: an approach associated with Ornette Coleman in which the music contains improvised solos free of preset chord progressions and sometimes free of preset meter.

Field Hollers: communication between the enslaved with bended tones and slurs.

Form: the architecture of music.

Genres: a category of artistic composition, as in music or literature, characterized by similarities in form, style, or subject matter.

Gospel Music: the inheritance of African American folk traditions that emerged as a blues-influenced religious style around the late 1920s.

Great Migration: the movement of over six million African Americans from the rural Southern United States to urban areas in the North and West between 1916 and 1970, seeking better economic opportunities and escaping racial segregation.

Griot: storytellers who maintain a tradition of oral history in parts of West Africa.

Hard Bop: Jazz style of the late 1950s that continued through the 1960s.

Harmony: is the sound created by multiple notes played or sung simultaneously.

Hemiola: a rhythmic technique where a musical phrase or passage is written in a meter that conflicts with the prevailing meter, often creating a 3:2 ratio, where three notes are played in the time of two, producing a complex and intriguing rhythmic effect.

Hip Hop: a genre of popular music that emerged in the mid-1970s in New York City. The term hip-hop music is sometimes used synonymously with the term rap music. The genre is characterized by stylized rhythmic sounds, often built around dance grooves, electronic drumbeats, and rapping, a percussive vocal delivery of rhymed poetic speech as consciousness-raising expression.

Improvisation is a key element in African American music genres, allowing musicians to express themselves in the moment creatively.

Jazz: is a uniquely American music and one of America's original art forms. It originated in the African American communities of New Orleans, Louisiana, in the late 1800s and early 1900s, from blues and ragtime music.

Measure: refers to a time segment within a piece of music defined by a fixed number of beats—vertical bar lines separate measures.

Melody: is a single line of notes heard in succession as a coherent unit.

Meter: refers to the rhythmic grouping of beats, indicating the organization of music through time. Meter defines the pattern of strong and weak beats within a measure, creating a rhythmic pulse that guides the music's flow.

Middle Passage: the journey of enslaved Africans across the Atlantic Ocean during the TransAtlantic Slave Trade.

Minstrelsy: was a type of staged theatrical entertainment whereby white performers, with faces darkened by burnt cork, entertained their audiences with exaggerated depictions of slave life.

Percussion: the heavy use of drums, rattles, bells, and other rhythmic instruments.

Player: a person who plays without written music.

Polyrhythms: a prominent feature of African music, where multiple rhythms are played simultaneously, is often present in African American music.

Polyphonic Harmonies: the use of multiple melodies at the same time.

Poly-metric Structures: Different instruments are playing simultaneously in different meters.

Progression: refers to a sequence of chords played in a specific order that forms the harmonic foundation of a piece.

Ragging: Changing the melody line by syncopation or other effects.

Ragtime: is a piano style of music that came into existence shortly after the Civil War.

Rhythm: is the movement of music in time.

Ring Shout: was a type of ceremonial dance in which the participants gathered in the middle of the floor and, with the start of the spiritual, moved or shuffled around in a circle.

Scat Singing: jazz improvisation using the human voice as an instrument, with nonsense syllables instead of words.

Slave Ship: a ship transporting enslaved people, especially one carrying enslaved people from Africa.

Spirituals: are the earliest body of vernacular folk literature that expresses the religious feeling of African Americans.

Swing: a word denoting the feeling projected by a jazz performance which successfully combines constant tempo, syncopation, eighth notes, rhythmic lilt, liveliness, and rhythmically cohesive group playing.

Syncopation: accenting rhythmic patterns on weak beats rather than strong beats.

Third Stream: a term used to describe a fusion of jazz improvisation with the instrumentation and compositional forms of classical music.

Timeline Patterns: Recurring rhythmic phrases that provide a foundation for improvisation.

Work Songs: songs that expressed the mundane experiences of the people. The text of work songs generally mirrored the unfair conditions African Americans lived and labored under.

12/8 Bell Pattern: a rhythmic pattern commonly found in Afro-Cuban music.

BIBLIOGRAPHY

Allen, W. F., Ware, C. P., & Garrison, L. M. (1995). *Slave songs of the United States*. Dover Publications. (Original work published 1867)

Armstrong, L. (1986). *Satchmo: My life in New Orleans*. Prentice-Hall Press.

Balliett, W. (1977). *Improvising: Sixteen jazz musicians and their art*. Oxford University Press.

Baraka, A. (1963). *Blues people: The Negro experience in white America and the music that developed from it*. William Morrow.

Baraka, A. (1967). *Black American music*. William Morrow.

Barker, D. (1986). *A life in jazz* (A. Shipton, Ed.). Oxford University Press.

Barz, G. (2004). *Music in East Africa: Experiencing music, expressing culture*. Oxford University Press.

Berlin, E. (1980). *Ragtime: A musical and cultural history*. University of California Press.

Berliner, P. (1984). *Thinking in jazz: The infinite art of improvisation*. University of Chicago Press.

Bloom, H. (2003). *The Harlem Renaissance*. Chelsea House Publishing.

Boyer, H. C. (1979). Contemporary gospel music—Part 1: Sacred or secular. *Black Perspective in Music, 7*(1), 5–58.

Boyer, H. C. (1995). *The golden age of gospel.* University of Illinois Press.

Brown, C. T. (1983). *The art of rock and roll.* Prentice-Hall.

Brown, J., & Tucker, B. (1986). *James Brown: The Godfather of Soul.* Macmillan.

Carlin, B. (2007). *The birth of the banjo: Joel Walker Sweeney and early minstrelsy.* McFarland & Company.

Celestan, K. (2018). *Freedom's dance: Social, aid and pleasure clubs in New Orleans* (Photographs by E. Waters). Louisiana State University Press.

Chilton, J. (1994). *Let the good times roll: The story of Louis Jordan and his music.* University of Michigan Press.

Crawford, R. (2001). *An introduction to America's music.* W. W. Norton & Company.

Douglass, F. (1962). *Life and times of Frederick Douglass, written by himself* (Original work published 1881). Collier Books.

Dubois, L. (2016). *The banjo: America's African instrument.* Harvard University Press.

Du Bois, W. E. B. (1967). *The souls of Black folk: Essays and sketches* (Original

    work published 1903; Diamond Jubilee ed.). Fisk University Press.

Ellington, E. K. "Duke." (1980). *Music is my mistress*. DaCapo Press. (Original

    work published 1973)

Elliott, D. (1995). *Music matters: A philosophy of music education*. Oxford

    University Press.

Ellison, R. (1964). *Shadow and act*. Penguin Books.

Epstein, D. (2004). *Sinful tunes and spirituals: Black folk music to the Civil

    War*. University of Illinois Press.

Feather, L. (1988). *The encyclopedia of jazz*. Horizon Press.

Feather, L. (1984). *From Satchmo to Miles*. DaCapo Press. (Original work

    published by Stein and Day)

Floyd, S. A., Jr. (1995). *The power of Black American music: Interpreting its

    history from Africa to the United States*. Oxford University Press.

Fox, T. (1983). *Showtime at the Apollo*. Holt, Rinehart and Winston.

Freire, P. (2009). *Pedagogy of the oppressed*. Continuum International.

Garvey, M. (2020). *Message to the people: The course of African philosophy*.

    Dover Publications.

Gates, H. L., Jr. (1988). *The signifying monkey: A theory of Afro-American literary criticism*. Oxford University Press.

Gillespie, D. (1979). *To be or not to bop: Memoirs* (With A. Frazer). Doubleday.

Gioia, T. (2021). *The history of jazz*. Oxford University Press.

Gitler, I. (1985). *Swing to bop: An oral history of the transition in jazz in the 1940s*. Oxford University Press.

Guralnick, P. (1986). *Sweet soul music: Rhythm and blues and the southern dream of freedom*. Harper & Row.

Handy, W. C. (1941). *Father of the blues: An autobiography* (A. Bontemps, Ed.). Sedgwick & Jackson.

Hardie, D. (2001). *The loudest trumpet*. toExcel.

Haskins, J. (1977). *The Cotton Club*. Random House.

Haydon, G. (2002). *Quintet of the year*. Aurum Press Ltd.

Heilbut, A. (1997). *The gospel sound: Good news and bad times*. Limelight Editions.

Johnson, J. W. (Ed.). (1922). *The book of American Negro poetry*. Harcourt, Brace.

Jost, E. (1975). *Free jazz*. Universal Edition.

King, M. L., Jr. (1967). *Where do we go from here: Chaos or community?*

Harper & Row.

Kingsbury, P. (Ed.). (1998). *The encyclopedia of country music.* Oxford

University Press.

Locke, A. (1968). *The Negro and his music: Negro art, past and present.*

Kennikat Press.

Louisville Story Program. (2024). *I'm glad about it.* Louisville Story Program.

Lovell, J. (1986). *Black song: The forge and the flame. The story of how the Afro-*

American spirituals was hammered out. Paragon House.

Marquis, D. M. (2005). *In search of Buddy Bolden: First man of jazz.*

Louisiana State University Press.

Marsalis, B. (2023). *Black American music Footprints podcast with Mondre*

Moffett. SSCLiveTV. https://www.ssclivetv.org

McCarthy, A. J. (1974). *Big band jazz.* Putman's Sons.

Moffett, M. (2019). *An improvising curriculum for jazz music.* LAP

LAMBERT Academic Publishing.

Monsom, I. (1996). *Saying something: Jazz improvisation and interaction.*

University of Chicago Press.

Murray, A. (1976). *Stomping the blues*. McGraw-Hill.

Nissen, P. (2014). *Buddy Bolden's Storyville blues*. Lulu.

https://www.lulu.com

Palmer, R. (1981). *Deep blues*. The Viking Press.

Porter, L. (1998). *John Coltrane: His life and music*. The University of

Michigan Press.

Price, S. (1990). *What do they want? A jazz autobiography*. University of

Illinois Press.

Reagon, B. J. (Ed.). (1992). *We'll understand it better by and by: Pioneering*

African American gospel composers. Smithsonian Institution Press.

Southern, E. (1997). *The music of Black Americans: A history* (3rd ed.). W. W.

Norton.

Stewart, E. L. (1998). *African American music: An introduction*. Schirmer

Books.

Tanner, P. (2005). *Jazz*. McGraw-Hill.

Turner, R. B. (2009). *Jazz religion, the second line, and Black New Orleans*.

Indiana University Press.

Toll, R. C. (1974). *Blacken up: The minstrel show in nineteenth-century America*. Oxford University Press.

Wald, E. (2004). *Escaping the Delta*. HarperCollins Publishers.

Work, J. W. (1940). *American Negro songs and spirituals*. Crown Publishers.

www.ingramcontent.com/pod-product-compliance
Lightning Source LLC
Chambersburg PA
CBHW051523120626
46551CB00012B/1058